Permaculture in **POTS**

How to Grow Food in Small Urban Spaces

Juliet Kemp

D0770833

Permanent Publications

Published by

Permanent Publications
Hyden House Ltd
The Sustainability Centre
East Meon
Hampshire GU32 1HR
England
Tel: 01730 823 311
Fax: 01730 823 322
Overseas: (international code +44 - 1730)
Email: enquiries@permaculture.co.uk
Web: www.permaculture.co.uk

Published in association with

Permaculture Association (Britain), BCM Permaculture Association, London WC1N 3XX
Tel: 0845 458 1805 or + 44 0113 2307461
Email: office@permaculture.org.uk Web: www.permaculture.org.uk

Designed by Two Plus George, www.TwoPlusGeorge.co.uk

Printed in the UK by Cambrian Printers, Aberystwyth, Wales

All paper from FSC certified mixed sources

The Forest Stewardship Council (FSC) is a non-profit international
organisation established to promote the responsible management of the
world's forests. Products carrying the FSC label are independently certified
to assure consumers that they come from forests that are managed to meet
the social, economic and ecological needs of present and future generations.

British Library Cataloguing-in-Publication Data
A catalogue record for this book is available from the British Library
ISBN 978 1 85623 097 1

CONTENTS

ABOUT THE AUTHOR

Juliet Kemp lives in London with her partner, dog, and baby son. She has recently acquired a (very small) garden and a new north-facing garden (two whole new permaculture designs to plan and execute!), and still does plenty of container growing.

When not writing (fiction or non-fiction) or pottering about her plant-growing spaces, she enjoys cycling, climbing, knitting, and making/upcycling things generally. After several years of learning about and using permaculture, she completed the Permaculture Design Course at the Earth Activist Training 2011 course, which she found incredibly inspiring.

She has a website at http://julietkemp.com

INTRODUCTION

WHY TRY PERMACULTURE IN POTS?

So, why grow your own food? Growing your own food, even only a little of it, is fun in and of itself – plus you get very tasty results! It's good for your mental wellbeing, and if you do it right, it's good for the planet as well. It's hard to underestimate the satisfaction of eating something you've grown yourself; and just messing around with earth and seeing seeds sprout and turn into plants is a rewarding and sometimes even magical experience. In urban areas, many of us have very little regular contact with the natural environment; growing a few plants in pots is an easy and fun way of getting back in touch with nature and natural processes, even within the concrete jungle.

But why permaculture? Permaculture is a way of doing things – whether that's growing food, constructing communities, or anything else – which focuses on creating a sustainable, self-reliant system, and a sustainable human environment. It's a great way of making sure that when you create your garden, you're working in environmentally beneficial and sustainable ways – and sustaining yourself at the same time.

As a concept, permaculture can be applied to a huge range of situations and human activity, but it first arose from ideas around plant systems: aiming to create a way of growing food that is sustainable, productive, and which works with the environment (both in the broadest sense and in the very local sense of the space in which you're growing things) rather than against it. It's an appealing way to work: as a gardener, working with the plants, yourself, and your space to create a system in which all of the pieces can fit comfortably together.

Urban Permaculture

A permaculture approach can be particularly useful in urban areas, where you have many more constraints. If all you have is a paved area, you can still grow vegetables in pots or other containers, but that does mean that your system will operate slightly differently from if you were growing in the ground. Using a permaculture perspective will allow you to observe and consider *your* space and situation, and make decisions accordingly. A south-facing balcony with a concrete wall at the back could be an excellent home for warmth loving fruit and tomato plants; a north-facing roof garden will need something different. The pots may in some ways limit your space, but they also make it easy to move plants around to experiment and find out how you can get the most out of the various plants. Permaculture is also about making the most of the available space (see p.15), using edges, height, and companion growing. Thinking about yourself and your space as a holistic system can even help you save money – for example, by setting up worm composting (see p.33) to make your own compost rather than having to buy it in every year.

Thinking about permaculture when setting up your garden makes it possible to create the best and most sustainable system you can, working in harmony with the environment you're given and making the most of all your available resources. That makes sense wherever you're growing, but it makes even more sense in a small urban environment where you want to maximise output from a small space.

This introduction will cover some of the principles of permaculture, as I talk about planning, practicalities, and the structure of the rest of the book.

The Structure of this Book

The rest of the Introduction will cover the basics for getting started: planning your space with reference to permaculture principles; how to maximise your space; and the practicalities (like water, pots, and compost) that you'll need to think about.

The remainder of the book is arranged month-by-month: wherever you are in the year, open the book at that chapter, and it'll tell you what you should be doing. (See the end of this Introduction for a quick note on how to use this book in different climate zones and seasons, if you're not in the UK.)

Each chapter will start off with an overview of what was going on in my own urban container garden that month, and a list of things you

My south-facing balcony at the height of summer.

3

should be doing in that month. Here's what to expect in the rest of the chapters.

CHAPTER 1 NOVEMBER

Overwintering beans and peas; creating your own compost and leaf mould; a green tomato chutney recipe to preserve any remaining tomatoes; building a cold frame; winter herbs; and tidying up ready for the next season. The herb of the month is sage.

CHAPTER 2 DECEMBER

Protecting plants from the cold (and which ones don't need protection); using chickweed (a prolific and very useful weed!); and what you can harvest for your Christmas dinner (and as post-Christmas medication) from your space. The herb of the month is thyme.

CHAPTER 3 JANUARY

How to get hold of seeds (by saving, swapping, and making cuttings); planning your space and your growing season; and the opportunities for growing fruit in pots. The herb of the month is rosemary.

CHAPTER 4 FEBRUARY

Succession sowing; early vegetables to get started; frost dates and how to manage frost problems; starting seeds off; and making self-watering containers. The herb of the month is parsley.

CHAPTER 5 MARCH

Revitalising your old compost; what to do with your successfully over-wintered plants now the weather is picking up; more information about planting out and hardening off peas and beans; all the details about lettuce and chillies, peppers, aubergines, carrots, spinach beet and chard; and growing potatoes in containers. The herb of the month is oregano.

CHAPTER 6 APRIL

How to grow tomatoes, courgettes, and strawberries; making the most of your space as the containers start to stack up; and companion planting to discourage insects. The herb of the month is chives.

CHAPTER 7 MAY

Growing microgreens and baby greens; dealing ethically and organically with pests; and guerrilla gardening to use spare seeds and seedlings. The herb of the month is savoury.

CHAPTER 8   JUNE
Midsummer and the problem of bolting; how water affects different plants at different stages; and thinning and pinching out carrots, greens, and tomatoes. The herb of the month is basil.

CHAPTER 9   JULY
Propagating strawberries; and starting to think about crops for autumn. The herb of the month is Fennel.

CHAPTER 10   AUGUST
Harvesting, eating, and preserving the food you've been growing, with information on preserving veg and some fabulous recipes; more on saving seed; and planting potatoes for your Christmas dinner! The herb of the month is mint.

CHAPTER 11   SEPTEMBER
Bringing delicate herbs like basil inside for the winter; autumn greens; and foraging and wild jellies. The herb of the month is yarrow.

CHAPTER 12   OCTOBER
Tidying up at the end of the season; plants you can keep on sowing through October; setting up the cold frame; and useful weeds that can still be harvested at this time of year (like dandelion roots). The herb of the month isn't a herb, it's a spice, ginger!

Finally, **CHAPTER 13 ZONES 4 AND 5** talks about the wider urban environment and its possibilities. These include guerrilla gardening, urban foraging (in many guises!); how to get yourself about the place in a permaculture-friendly way, and interacting with the other people around you to improve your local food network.

There's also a brief Appendix with a few useful websites, information resources, and seed providers, as well as plans for any built structure that appears in the book (such as the cold frame on p.36), and sample plans for different sizes and types of paved urban space.

Planning your Space

There are a few general things to consider when planning your space; the first being the general advantages and disadvantages of container gardening.

Urban Container Gardening

Advantages and problems

The biggest advantage of gardening on a balcony or patio is closeness to the house.

There's an old Chinese proverb that says, "the best fertiliser is the gardener's shadow". Basically, the more often you visit your plants, the better your crop will be. You'll be able to fix problems more readily, as well as making the most of your potential crop by harvesting as things become ready. With cut-and-come-again plants in particular (see p.90), this can significantly boost your crop. In permaculture, this area is referred to as zone 1 (see p.8), and is where you put all the plants which need the most regular attention. So while, as urban container gardeners, our available area may be small, it's very valuable, and it can be much more productive than you'd expect.

A big advantage of gardening in containers is that pots are portable. Even if you're renting, you can set up a garden with the security that if you move, your garden can come with you; avoiding the fear that you'll lose all your hard work if you move at the wrong time of year. Container gardening also enables you to make use of the 'low maintenance' paved spaces that are increasingly common in urban homes (especially rented ones) and which may be your only available outside space if you're living, as many urban dwellers are, in a flat.

The main disadvantage you'll face is that container gardening doesn't have the same self-sustainability that gardening in the ground does. The soil needs more attention, since there are few or no microorganisms in there to generate fertility. Even if you were growing plants in the ground you would need to add fertile matter, but it's even more important to do this when container gardening. One of the aims of this book is to help you to make your container gardening as self-sustaining as possible – but doing that does require more input from you! By choosing plants carefully, setting up composting, and where possible making your own fertiliser, it's possible to make the most of the resources available within the system, and minimise what you need to import. The good news is that the independence of your containers does reduce the amount of weeding you'll need to do!

Containers are also more prone to drying out (and depending on your space, won't always get rained on – mine don't, due to the overhanging balcony of the next flat up), so you need to water more often than you might with a regular garden. Having said that, one great option for reducing watering which isn't available to those growing straight in the soil is to use self-watering containers (see how to guide on p.73 to make these). In general, however, there's a bit less room for error and for the plants to look after themselves than there is in a more traditional garden; so you the gardener will need to do a little more.

You may also have problems with plants that need insect fertilisation, as beneficial insects may not make it to your plot, especially if you're growing on a high up balcony or roof garden. There are ways of encouraging them (see p.116) and alternative solutions (see p.112 for a discussion of hand-fertilising courgettes), but it's worth being aware of the potential problem when deciding what you want to grow. You may prefer simply to avoid plants (such as courgettes) which require insect fertilisation. I'll flag up these plants as they occur in the book – luckily there aren't too many of them so you won't be too restricted.

You may well find that you have your very own microclimate, which can be both an advantage or a disadvantage. A south-facing balcony on a concrete block (my own setup) will be significantly warmer than a patch of regular ground in the same geographical area. This is great for growing tender plants such as tomatoes and peppers, which will love the heat and light; but pots will dry out faster and some plants may find the heat a bit too much in midsummer. Peas, for example, will stop cropping sooner than those in a slightly cooler spot. Alternatively, a north-facing area will be cooler, shadier, and choosing plants will be a little more difficult (see p.60 for more on this).

Considering safety

This isn't a major problem on a patio, but if you're putting containers on a balcony or a windowsill, there are a couple of important safety considerations.

Firstly, how much weight can your balcony bear? A solid concrete balcony will be able to cope with a lot more than a flimsier iron one. Err on the side of caution, and remember that pots that have recently been watered can be very heavy. If you're concerned about weight, look at plastic pots rather than ceramic ones (see p.17 for a discussion of containers). However, remember that your balcony ought to be rated for a couple of people's worth of weight, so don't worry too much! If you're using a roof, you need to calculate the total weight it can carry – again, if in doubt, err on the side of caution. You can consult a builder or surveyor if you're unsure.

The other important issue is securing containers properly. Having a container full of plants and wet compost land on someone's head as they walk past could be disastrous. If everything's on the inside of the railings, this is fine, as the fall will be short and only onto your toes! The big problem is when you either put a container on top of a railing, or hang it over the edge of one. Make sure that it can't be knocked off or blown loose; also keep an eye on the fixings and check them regularly for damage or signs of ageing. If you have children, consider their heights and the tendency to pull at things.

You'll need to think about how you want to lay the containers out before you affix them; so let's look next at how you go about planning your space.

Permaculture Principles: How to apply them when planning your space

The basic principles of permaculture are a good starting point when planning your space (see opposite).

Zones

An important permaculture idea is that of zones – different areas at different distances from the house. As already mentioned, an urban space is likely to be very close to the house, in zone 1. (Zone 0 is the house itself, which you will probably use for starting off some seeds and for growing some very delicate plants, especially over winter; and zone 2 is for less intensively grown and hardier vegetables, typically being an allotment or similar space in an urban area.) This as a rule would imply

Permaculture Principles

Various permaculture designers and writers have come up with different lists of principles, but these are a reasonable summary of the basics:

1. Observe before you act, and make decisions for your specific site and situation.

2. Plan with consideration for how the space will be used; think about zones and networks.

3. Connect the parts of the design – better connected ecosystems are healthier and more diverse.

4. Catch and store energy and materials; create cycles rather than losing energy.

5. Each part of the design should have multiple functions, and each function be supported by multiple methods.

6. Embrace diversity to create a better supported system. The most diverse part of a system is the edge, so consider that and optimise it.

7. Design in multiple dimensions to maximise diversity and connection.

8. Start small and expand out as you succeed; change as little as you need in order to get an effect.

9. Use problems (and mistakes!) as solutions, to inspire your decisions.

that it is best used for plants that you use regularly and which benefit most from regular attention – herbs and salad vegetables, in particular.

However, if this is your only growing space, you will of course think about it differently from if you also have an allotment down the road. You may well want to include a few plants that you'd normally expect to grow further away.

From a practical point of view, it makes most sense to grow things that you like, and that are either expensive to buy, or simply taste better fresh. (This last is not hard; nearly everything does.) Rocket, for example, is great to grow in pots, and the difference between fresh rocket and the bleach washed stuff out of a supermarket packet is incredible. (See p.84 for information on growing lettuce and rocket.)

Multiple Crops

Given the limited nature of urban container spaces, one way to make the most of what space you do have is to grow plants that produce more than a single crop. Fruiting plants – peas and beans, as well as tomatoes, blueberries, strawberries, or raspberries – will carry on producing fruit over a period of weeks, continuing to produce more as you harvest them. These can be really valuable for a small area. Similarly, cut-and-come-again vegetables like rocket, some types of lettuce, and chard, will continue to crop over weeks or even months. (I've had chard plants that kept growing straight through winter and were cropping for over a year all told before they went to seed.) Carrots or other root vegetables, on the other hand, grow only one root per plant. Once you've harvested that, that's your lot. As such, they're quite space intensive for the output you get. Of course, you may want to grow some root veg – young carrots are very suitable for pot growing (see p.88) and taste great, and potatoes can be grown very successfully in containers (see p.103). But the smaller your space, the more it makes sense to maximise yield by choosing multi-cropping plants. Happily, these also tend to be the plants which are easiest to grow well, because you, as the gardener, are working with the inclination of the plant to produce fruit or leaves.

Flows

Sun, shade, wind, and frost

An important concept in permaculture is that of flow; looking at the different sorts of things that move through a given space. These include sun, wind, water, and frost/temperature, which are all forms of energy, but also the movement of people through and within the space. You need, therefore, to think about the natural environment and natural cycles that move through your space.

Sunshine and shadow

One of the most important flows within your space is that of the sun and shade, and the patterns they fall in.

Watch your space for at least a day (ideally, you'd make observations over the course of a year, as the angle of the sun changes with the seasons) and see where the sun is at various times. How many hours of sunlight do you get? Do you notice this changing at different times of year?

You can get away with only doing this for six months if you pick the right six months – the sun from 21(ish) June (the summer solstice) to 21(ish) December (the winter solstice) is the same as the sun from 21(ish) December to 21(ish) June, just in reverse. A week after the summer solstice, the sun's height and path will be about the same as it was a week before the summer solstice, so one observation will do the job for both.

If you don't want to wait and observe for a full year, or even for six months, you can work the basics out by looking at the direction your space faces in, and noting the shade patterns for at least one day.

Broadly speaking, south-facing means plenty of sunlight; but south-facing walls can get very hot, so although the sun is good for vegetables, you'll need to be vigilant with the watering (and/or use self-watering containers, as on p.73). A west-facing space will get the afternoon and evening sun, and west-facing walls tend to be slightly sheltered. 'West is Best' is an old gardeners' maxim – west-facing is kinder to plants than south-facing, which can be a bit extreme. South-facing is great, however, if you want to grow tender plants like peppers and citrus, which will love the heat. East-facing walls will get the morning sun, but tend to experience temperature extremes and potentially cold winds.

North-facing walls will get no sun in the winter, and only an hour or two in midsummer, so you'll need to choose shade loving plants, and you may struggle to grow many traditional vegetables at all. You may be better looking for alternative, often perennial, plants that will do well in pots and which tolerate shade. Check out pp.60-61 for suggestions for a north-facing space, or look through the book *Plants For A Future* to find suggestions for less usual shade tolerant edibles.

It's also important to look at how the shadows fall. If your space is south-facing but directly to the south is a much taller building, you'll get a lot less sun than you might otherwise expect. Buildings, trees and walls can all cast significant shadows.

It's understandable and perfectly reasonable to want to go straight ahead with your first crops without extensive observation beforehand. One of the advantages of container gardening is that you're not committing yourself to anything: you can always move the pots later! You should however keep a careful eye on the space over your first year of growing, and if possible keep records of where the sun and shade fall in your plot, and how many hours of sunshine you get, to inform decisions and planning in future years. In fact, records are always worth keeping, even after the first year, so you can look back to see what worked well and what didn't.

Wind and water flows

Once you've got an idea of which parts of your space are in sun and in shadow, and for how long in a day, you can think about wind and water flows. Balconies, patios, and windowsills are often at least a little sheltered from the wind, which may well mean that you can plant slightly more delicate plants than you might in a more exposed space, and have them survive. However, if your space regularly has a howling gale whistling through it, you'll need to stick to tougher plants.

Water flow is less of an issue for container gardens than it is for gardening in the ground, as you'll expect to have to water your pots yourself anyway, and the water won't flow as well through the pots as it would in the ground. However, you do still need to consider water flow within the pots – make sure that they drain well in the winter so the roots of your plants won't rot, and consider using saucers under pots in the summer to make the most of the water you do put in there. Water is discussed in more depth on p.24.

People

Finally, there's people-flow to consider. As it is a small space, it may be that people don't often move through the area, but you do want to think about how you will be able to move within it (can you access all the pots you're planning to put in, in order to water, tie back, harvest, etc?), and also other ways in which people might want to use the space.

Polyculture and Diversity

Diversity is important, even in a small space. If you grow only one thing, you're much more vulnerable to loss of an entire group (e.g. if caterpillars descend on your lettuce). Gardening on a small scale is really good for diversity, as you'll probably want to grow lots of different sorts of plants (although in my south-facing space I do have a bit of a mania for tomatoes!). Companion planting (where you grow different plants together which are beneficial to one another – often this is intended to deter pests) is also great for small spaces (see p.122) as another way of maximising your potential crop.

Perennial Plants

Perennial plants are plants which continue cropping from year to year, as opposed to annuals, which only last for a single year. Most familiar vegetables in the Western diet are annuals, although most fruit plants are perennial, as is asparagus and globe artichoke. Perennials have significant advantages over annuals. They're less work, as once established they will just keep on cropping with little need for the gardener to do anything (and certainly no need to keep replanting year on year). They often start cropping earlier in the spring than annuals do, because they don't have to grow themselves up from seed. And they're often more pest- and disease-resistant, due to having more stored strength and so being able to bounce back from an attack where an annual would turn up its roots and expire. Here are a few suggestions for perennial vegetables that can do well in containers:

- Many herbs are perennial, including rosemary, thyme, chives and mint (notable exceptions are basil and dill). Check the end of each chapter of this book for information on specific herbs.

- Strawberries are perennial, although only last for a couple of years.

- If you want green salad leaves, sorrel, watercress, mitsuba, and Turkish rocket are all perennial and do well in pots. Chicory is also perennial but the flavour deteriorates in the second and subsequent leaves, so it may be better to encourage it to self-seed instead.

- Daubenton's kale and nine star broccoli are perennial brassicas which may be worth trying in large pots. I haven't grown nine star broccoli at all, and have grown Daubenton's kale only on my allotment. From its spread there I'd suggest using an 45cm wide pot. It is worth a go, though – hardy, tasty, and keeps growing all winter! It's fairly tolerant of shade as well.

- Tree onions (also known as Egyptian onions and walking onions) are perennials which grow little bulbs (known as top sets) at the top of their stalks. You can harvest these (note that they won't usually appear in the plant's first year) in late summer, or leave them to bend over, hit the ground, root, and produce a new plant! The bulbs in the ground can also be harvested, but leave enough in the ground to grow the next year's crop. Welsh onion is another option, but is more like a spring onion or chive.

Alongside perennial fruit, herbs, and vegetables, you can also look into self-seeding veg (such as rocket) which will also tend to need less intensive care than less vigorous annuals. I've mentioned in the rest of the book when a plant is a good self-seeder.

Multi-dimensional Design

Another important aspect of permaculture is the idea of multi-dimensional design. Permaculture is heavily informed by the concept of the forest garden, and forests are strongly layered (especially at the edges) so that different plants can co-exist and take advantage of the different heights. An urban paved space is ideal for this – you can grow differently tall plants, but you can also stack your containers at different heights, either by creating shelves or holders, or by attaching them to walls or balconies. Think about whether you can grow some lettuce at the bottom of your peas; or whether you can fit an extra pot in underneath an existing one. Think of your space in three dimensions, not just in two, and work out how you can use it to the best advantage. Time can also be seen as a dimension. The next section covers this more in-depth.

Not just for the Plants…

You may also need to think about other things that live in your space – some kind of storage for pots, tools, and seeds; a wormery for compost (see p.33); or a couple of chairs for when you want to sit out in the summer sunshine. This is part of considering your relationship with the space: permaculture is about creating sustainable systems in *all* senses. Creating a space that you enjoy spending time in and that is capable of sustaining you mentally as well as physically is just as important as creating a space that will sustain your plants. Not only that, but creating a space you enjoy spending time in will in fact sustain your plants as well, as the more time you spend around the plants, the more likely you are to notice what they need and provide it.

As well as thinking about your own interaction with the plants, think about their interaction with each other – consider the three dimensional nature of your space (discussed below), and whether you might be able to make use of companion planting (see p.122).

Planning to Maximise your Space

With a small space, you really need to ensure that you make the most of what space you do have. This fits in well with the multi-dimensional design principle.

We normally think first about the horizontal; how many plants or containers we can fit into the available floor space. But just as important is to consider the vertical space available.

There are a couple of ways of looking at this. One is to consider the edges of your space – do you have walls or fences? Can you use these to grow plants up? Climbing plants like peas and beans (p.82) or berry canes (such as raspberries and blackberries, see p.62) will particularly benefit from this. You will also need to consider which direction the wall or fence faces. South, west, or east-facing walls can all be useful. North-facing walls are likely to be very shady.

Walls can help to protect plants from the effects of the wind (peas will do well against a wall), and a wall may also help create its own micro-climate. Victorian kitchen gardeners would train peaches up brick walls to benefit from the heat storage capacity of the brick. Modern house walls can work just as well for this, so if you're trying out something like a citrus tree (see p.65), siting it by a south- or west-facing wall is ideal, and will give it more warmth (reflected from the wall) as well as protecting it from the wind.

Another possibility for maximising space is to find a way of stacking pots, for example on shelves of various sorts. A shelving unit with plenty of space for growing plants between the shelves can make a massive increase in your available space. You may be able to get hold of a reusable one from websites like Freecycle, or from a local office which is redecorating. Small stepladders can provide stacked shelving, or you can construct something similar from wood (skipped or otherwise). Alternatively you can make your own more minimal version of this, using planks (often available from nearby skips) and bricks or even up-ended tin cans. I used a couple of polystyrene containers as the supports for one of my shelves. You may not want to build these high enough to put a pot entirely underneath, but the height increase will still make a little more space for a pot that goes next to the shelf, as the widest parts of the pots will be at different heights. You'll also find it easier to get at all of the pots than you would if they were all on the floor.

If you have a balcony with a railing, you may be able to attach pots or troughs to it. (As discussed above, do be careful to make sure they are securely attached.) You could even, if the railing is sufficiently solid, put a trough on top and suspend another one to the inside (the outside will be difficult to get at). If hanging pots from the inside of a railing, bear in mind that they may overshadow plants underneath them; but also that any water runoff will go into the plants beneath, which can be helpful.

Similarly, hanging baskets can be very useful when trying to increase your space. They can be hung from a railing, from a wall, or even from a ceiling, if you are in a block of flats and have another balcony directly above you. Strawberries can grow very well in hanging baskets; of course, you can also grow pretty much anything else that you would grow in a small regular pot. I've used mine for marigolds, polyanthus and micro-greens; creeping thyme might also do well.

Finally, you can use height differences within a single pot. Plant rocket around the base of your rosemary bush, or lettuce at the base of your peas. Microgreens under tomatoes is another easy option. Bear in mind that the more plants you fit in one container, the more food and water it will need; but multiple plants can thrive quite happily in the same container, and you'll maximise the use of the compost and the pot footprint.

It's important, when stacking containers in various ways, to bear in mind the way in which the light will be affected. Pots on the lowest level of a shelf may be part shaded (so you might want to use those levels for plants like mint which do well in shade, see p.162). Shelves may cast a shadow on other areas of the space, unless they're stacked against a wall or fence. Walls also cast their own shadow. The shadows will move through the day with the sun, so may not be disastrous, but it's something to bear in mind when considering the needs of your plants. Think again about the forest garden structure, where the most productive area is at the edge, where plants at different heights can all catch the sun. You can use your walls and railings to mimic a forest edge, and stack plants at different heights against those boundaries.

Time is the final dimension that you can consider. The most straight-forward way to use this is what's known as succession sowing: make several sowings of a particular type of seed at intervals of a couple of weeks, to maximise output. This works particularly well with plants like carrots, and with lettuces (it's good even for cut-and-come-again ones, which may bolt (go to seed) after a few weeks, but it's even more helpful if you're growing headed varieties). You can also use the same space for different crops at different times of the season. Plant a quick crop (microgreens, for example) in the spring in a pot that you later intend to use for a summer vegetable; or use your tomato plant pots for a quick crop of lettuce while the tomato seedlings are still getting themselves established indoors. Plant peas in the early spring, then when they die back, use the pot to transplant your courgette seedlings into. Experiment and see what works well for you! Again, if you're working your pots hard with multiple crops, be sure to feed regularly (see p.119).

Things to Obtain

Containers

You'll need some kind of container to grow your plants in, but there are plenty of alternatives to the easy but expensive option of visiting a garden centre and buying some. Not only is that expensive, it's also wasteful – there are plenty of things, especially those that would otherwise end up in the waste stream, that with a little imagination can be turned into containers for your plants. Here are some ideas for potentially useful containers:

- Old buckets (especially if they have holes in the bottom).

- Containers from restaurants – plastic pots that used to hold large quantities of mayonnaise or chutney, or 5 litre cooking oil drums. (wash these well!). If you ask at your local takeaway they may be happy to hand these over.

- Florists' buckets: if you go to your local florist, you can often get the black pots they use for display for a few pence each. See p.73 for instructions on how to turn these into self-watering containers.

- The large polystyrene containers that home-delivered frozen food (especially meat) is packed in. If you don't get home deliveries of frozen food, ask around your friends to see if anyone else does. (I get them from my parents, who have intermittent deliveries of organic frozen beef.)

- Plant pots that your friends or neighbours may have kicking around the garden shed that they don't use any more. Ask! Freecycle or Freegle (online groups where people can get rid of stuff they don't want for free; see the resources section for more info) are also good for this. You can either just keep an eye out for offers, or post to the group to ask if anyone has pots going spare.

- Old sinks (ceramic ones are attractive but very heavy). Old toilets can also be used to grow plants, but for a small space will probably take up more room than you want for not that much growing space.

- Cracked dustbins, as long as they're not so cracked that you'll lose soil from them. Small cracks are fine and even useful for drainage. However, do bear in mind that it takes a *lot* of soil to fill a large bin.

- Anything you happen to see in a nearby skip that will hold soil and which you can drill drainage holes in. Skips can be a great source of useful, reusable stuff (see p.187 for more on urban foraging). Be aware that technically taking anything from a skip is theft (yes, even though it's destined for landfill!). You may wish to check with the owner of the skip's contents before you take anything away (although in practice and in my experience it's

Marigolds growing in an old pair of Doc Martens hung from my balcony rail.

Old tyres used as containers, also hung to maximise vertical space. (Not mine, unfortunately – I spotted these near the Permaculture Garden at Glastonbury Festival.)

unlikely to be a problem if you just help yourself). Similarly, check out piles of rubbish in people's front gardens – but in this case definitely do ask before taking as one person's pile of rubbish is another's carefully collected stack of reusables.

- Old boots (yes, really – see photo above). The soil is quite hard to pack in, though, and you may want to pack out the toes with something else before putting the soil in.

- If you're up for a bit of basic carpentry, old pallets can be turned into square containers, with or without a bottom to them. You can adapt the instructions on p.36 for making a cold frame. These containers are likely to be at least medium size, so are better suited for a slightly larger space like a roof garden or patio.

Do be careful that you clean containers out thoroughly, especially if you don't know what has been in them previously. In most cases, you'll need to drill drainage holes in the bottom, to avoid your plants sitting in water and rotting their roots. If you have a container that's hard to drill holes in, you can provide drainage via about 5cm of pebbles or gravel in the bottom of each container. This does of course mean sourcing some gravel.

You also need to think about the size of your container. In general, go for bigger rather than smaller containers as smaller containers dry out faster. (See p.73 for suggestions on making self-watering containers.) Lettuces, rocket, and green leafy annual herbs can get by in 15cm deep containers (or even shallower for microgreens (see p.128; carrots, peppers, spinach and chard, and perennial herbs like rosemary need 23cm; and most other plants will want a 30cm deep container. In the sections on specific plants, I've suggested appropriate container sizes.

I've seen it suggested that many annuals can cope with 15cm deep containers, but in my experience they tend to struggle (especially if, as is often the case, your shallower containers are also smaller in width, meaning less soil, fewer nutrients, and less water retention). If in doubt, use a deeper container, as the soil will hold more water and more nutrients. In fact, in general you should use the biggest containers that you can get hold of, fill, and fit in your space. At the same time, experimenting with different sizes of container is fine, and if all you can get are 15cm pots, then by all means plant in those and be prepared to water more frequently and to stick to plants with smaller roots.

Compost

Far and away the best way to get compost is to make your own. Even on a balcony or patio you can produce your own compost via a wormery or a standalone composter (see p.32 for details). Sadly, compost doesn't happen overnight, so unless you're happy to start quite slowly, you may need to find other solutions to begin with.

There's evidence that green plant matter is actually more useful than topsoil when growing plants, so mixing that in with any compost you do have, or planting into green plant matter, is also worth experimenting with. However, to make this work well, you'll need to import some worms and other soil life to do the work of gradually turning it into soil, so it's not a good solution for small containers. If you have a bit more space and are able to make larger raised beds this is more feasible.

If you're starting from scratch, the easy but expensive way is to go to a garden centre and buy general purpose or potting compost by the bag. (Avoid peat compost, which is environmentally unsound, as extracting peat destroys a diverse and endangered ecosystem.)

Building Your Own Soil with Sheet Mulch

In his book, *Gaia's Garden*, Tony Hemenway recommends sheet mulching to create soil in the garden, and also mentions that he's seen the same technique used on pavements and rooftops. I haven't yet had a chance to try it, but I don't see why it shouldn't work in pots too! Note that you'll probably need a large container for this (though you could shift it out afterwards and start another lot), and you will need to import some worms and perhaps other insect life. You could do this straight onto the floor of your balcony or patio, but you won't then be able to take it with you if you move, and if you're renting, you may not be popular with the landlord. Here's the basic method, or see Hemenway's book for more info:

1. Lay down cardboard or newspapers (laid 3-13mm thick) and wet them thoroughly.

2. Add a thin layer of manure or fresh green clippings.

3. Add 20-30cm of loose straw, hay, leaves, seaweed, wood shavings, or any mixture of this sort of stuff. Add grass clippings or other green stuff if you're using wood shavings, to get the carbon/nitrogen balance right. Spray on water as you pile the material in; it should be damp but not wet.

4. Add 2.5-5cm of compost, soil, or easily compostable material like finely chopped kitchen waste. This is where you need to make sure, if using a pot, that you get some worms and other soil life in there. If you can get hold of a trowelful of decent soil, or compost, that will help with the soil life; worms can be acquired from a friend's garden, or bought online (see p.33 for more on worms and worm composting).

5. Top off with straw or fine bark as a mulch to suppress any weeds.

If you use actual compost in step 4, you can plant through the mulch directly into the compost. If you use kitchen waste, you'll need to give the worms a few weeks to turn it into something suitable for seeds to grow in.

Dedicated potting compost is available to buy by the bag, and if you're prepared to spend the money, it's the quickest way to get a decent soil mix. For most plants, general purpose compost is a bit too heavy, and if buying general purpose compost you'll need to mix it with some other things to get a soil that's best for your container plants. A good general purpose mix is as follows:

2 parts mature compost.
1 part vermiculite, to increase porosity.
1 part coarse sand (aka builders' sand), to ensure good drainage.
1 part coconut coir, to boost water retention.

For the 'compost' part of the mix, you can use your own worm compost, or general purpose garden centre compost. As a rule, a higher quantity of compost than this in the mix will tend to make it too dense and heavy, which will impact on the ability of the plants to get nutrition from it. It's also important that the mix should be able to retain plenty of water, as plants in pots are quicker to dry out than plants in the ground (see the Water section on pp. 24-26 for more on this). You should be able to tell by the feel of it how well your compost holds water. You also need to make sure that it's fairly fine, as plants find it harder to get nutrients from large lumps of compost (it will also affect the drainage).

Vermiculite is a natural mineral which helps to give the soil good structure and to retain moisture. Perlite (a form of volcanic glass) is another alternative which does roughly the same job. You can get organic versions of either of these. However, you may prefer to use a lower cost and less processed option. Try a little more sand, or old compost. I've never used vermiculite or perlite in my containers and have grown perfectly healthy plants.

If you have access to garden soil, or old compost, you can mix 1/3 new compost with 2/3 soil; or 1/3 new compost, and the rest a mix of old compost, sand, and coconut coir. See p.80 (March) for more on the possibilities of revitalising and reusing old compost.

It's fine to experiment with different substances and different mixes, and see how your plants do. And if you're aiming for lower cost options, a bit of experimentation may be your only option. Chopped straw is sometimes suggested as a low cost way of making compost a little lighter, so that may be worth trying. I've also sometimes mixed dry organic matter (that would otherwise go in the composter) directly in with new compost in a pot, with varying levels of success.

Finally, when making up your mix, remember that different plants do have slightly different requirements. Plants (such as most herbs) that prefer a lighter soil could use a little more sand in the mix; tomatoes may do quite well just in regular compost. If in doubt, however, stick with an all purpose mix as described above.

Council compost

Some councils generate compost from the food and green waste that they collect; this may be a cheaper option if it's available in your area. My local council, Southwark, sells this sort of compost at £4.50 for one 50l bag, or three bags for £12, which is good value. This compost is also about as ethical as it gets, being created from green waste that would otherwise go to landfill. Check your local council website, or contact your local waste recovery centre, to find out if they offer this. If they don't, write to your local councillor to find out why not!

Council compost tends to be much more solid and to have much larger chunks than general purpose compost. It doesn't hold water terribly well and tends to become very solid very quickly. It can be used as part of a mix, as above, but ideally you'd want to use it with another compost as well as mixed with the sand and other ingredients.

Horse manure

Another cheap option you can look for is horse manure, which is an excellent soil improver. Manure is harder to come by than it once was, but if you live anywhere near a stables (and even in a city this isn't impossible – there's a stables near me in Bermondsey) you can often get the stuff for free. However, unless it's very well composted (black with small particles) it's no good as a potting mix by itself. If you get hold of it after it's been rotting down for a while, use it as compost in a potting mix. Fairly new horse manure can instead be mixed with a little regular compost at the bottom of a large container and then covered with a more standard potting mix. Alternatively, you could fill a plastic bag with it and leave it in an unobtrusive corner somewhere, if you have the space, to rot down a bit further (ideally for a year) before you use it; or just add it to your regular composter. The other problem with fresh manure is that you are very likely to introduce some weeds along with the manure; by composting it down you reduce this likelihood. Adding it at the bottom of the container should also reduce the probability of weed spread. There is a small risk of *E. coli* from applying it directly, so if applying uncomposted manure, leave at least four months before harvesting vegetables that come into direct contact with the soil, and three months before harvesting fruit or vegetables that don't come into direct contact with the soil.

Water

Probably the biggest problem for container gardening is making sure that plants get enough water. If your plants ever run out of water (whatever that means for that plant; some plants need less water than others), even if they recover afterwards, it will mean that they do less well than if they had always had enough. Container dwelling plants can't just grow longer roots down into the ground to search for water, and containers tend to warm up faster than the ground, thus losing water more quickly. This is particularly true of ceramic or terracotta pots, which dry out very quickly in hot weather. You can ameliorate this a bit by making self-watering containers (see p.73), but you also need simply to make sure that you get enough water into your containers, of whatever sort, on a regular basis.

In urban areas, and especially if you live in a flat, options for collecting rainwater are likely to be limited, compared to house dwellers who can simply add a water butt to their property under the gutter drainpipe. However, if it's at all possible to harvest rainwater where you live, it's well worth it. Rainwater is better for your plants, as tap water is full of chlorine. It's also environmentally better to use rainwater as much as possible, rather than letting it run away down the drain and then using more tap water (harvested from rain elsewhere and piped over a not insignificant distance back to you!) for watering.

If you have a patio or roof garden, and you do have access to a drainpipe, sparing a corner to a water butt is well worth it. Get the biggest one that will fit into your space without taking too much growing room. Narrow space-saving waterbutts with a surprisingly high capacity are available. Put it up high enough (e.g. on bricks) to get a watering can under the tap at the bottom, direct the downpipe into it, and keep it covered to avoid losing water to evaporation. You can even grow plants on the top if it's short enough for you to reach up there, although a taller water butt will of course have a higher capacity. You'll also need to buy a kit that you fit into the drainpipe that will enable you to siphon some of the water off as it flows downwards, then redirect back to the downpipe when your water butt is full). This is important, as when your water butt fills up, you want it to overflow back into the drains, rather than all over your floor (potentially causing serious damage). In the UK, the amount of rain that falls on the roof of a 2-storey house over the course of a year is about enough to fill that entire 2-storey house, so the water butt, however large, *will* fill up at some point! Remember to check that interfering with the drainpipe won't get you into trouble with the landlord or building management, if you don't hold the freehold on the property.

Water butts can also be used, in some circumstances, to keep fish in, but this is beyond the scope of this book.

You can also simply leave a container open to the sky, which will collect any rain that falls on it. This is not as efficient as using a drainpipe, due to the reasonably small area involved, but it's better than nothing.

Unfortunately, in some cases you may not have access to the downpipe, and/or may be sufficiently overshadowed by other balconies that collecting rainwater simply isn't possible. This is the case for me; I've long considered some kind of Heath Robinson contraption leaning out from the balcony, but sadly this would breach my lease, not to mention being perhaps a little dangerous for those on the pavement below.

Another water saving option is to reuse bathwater or dish washing water, as long as you use biodegradable or natural washing up liquid and soap. If you plan to do this, use it quickly (as it can get a bit smelly). You can also look at getting a greywater diverter valve, which fits into your existing drainpipes and can divert your drain water off to a hose or container.

However, at least some of the time, even if you can use some rainwater or greywater, you're still likely to use tap water and a watering can; and that's fine. Certainly you shouldn't be put off growing plants if you need to use tap water! It is a bit more time consuming, as you have to go in and out more often, but functional (and you won't waste water when you have to lug it around yourself). If you have the space or opportunity, you can get into the habit of leaving tap water out for 24 hours before using it so that some of the chemicals off-gas. (This will also make drinking water taste better, in fact.) It's more important to get thirsty plants watered, though, so if you don't have any that's been standing out, that's fine.

Note that if your containers themselves are open to the rain, you'll need to make sure that they don't get waterlogged when it rains heavily, which will rot the roots of your plants. If you use a saucer to retain water (a good idea to avoid wasting water) in the summer, you'll need to take it away in the winter.

One of the best options for water saving, wherever you get your water from, is to use self-watering containers. See p.73 for a description of how to construct and use these.

Tools

Happily, you don't need very many tools for container gardening. A trowel is useful, but if you don't have one, you can use your hands to scoop compost out, or repurpose an old yoghurt pot as a scoop. Secateurs can also be handy when you're tidying up at the end of the season (when you may need to snip off or cut up dried stalks), but during the season,most things you want to cut or break can be done by pinching or at most using kitchen scissors for harvesting.

If you're growing vine tomatoes or peas, garden canes are the usual choice for providing support for the plants. You can also get standalone trellises, or wire cages, if you prefer. Another option for bush-type tomatoes is to grow them close together, and loop around them all a few times with string, so that they support each other. Garden canes are pretty cheap from a garden centre or perhaps your local pound shop, but you can also ask any friends with a garden if they can spare thin trimmed tree branches, or look for wind-blown branches in the park. (And, as above, keep an eye on local skips!)

Get a cheap notebook to record what you plant when, when you harvest and how much, and any other details you feel like noting. This will be incredibly helpful when it comes to planning the next season. However much you believe you'll remember what you did, you'll find that the details do fade.

Finally, you will definitely need some way of labelling your plants, or you'll have no idea what it is that's coming up there, and later on, which variety of tomato it was that has been doing so incredibly well. (I speak, unfortunately, from experience. I still don't know for certain which variety of cherry tomatoes I've been seed saving from for the last three years, but they're very tasty and seem to like it here!) Plastic or ceramic pot markers are available to buy; cheaper and reused alternatives include ice lolly sticks. I tried permanent marker on cut up bits of Tetrapak juice cartons one year; they're good for seed pots on the windowsill, but the marker faded too quickly in full sun and when being watered regularly, hence the tomato problem. Never put off labelling your plants, or you'll have forgotten by tomorrow morning which of the six seedling pots in front of you were beans and which were courgettes.

Transporting Things

One of the problems you may encounter if living in a city is how to transport things. Compost, for example, is heavy, and even if you make some of your own, you may well need to buy some in initially (see above). Pots can also be heavy, although there are other sorts of containers that you can use (see above). If you do need to transport heavy items, there are a number of choices:

- Order online with delivery – but make sure you're in at the right time! This, unfortunately, lets out cheap options like Freecycle, where the expectation is usually that you will collect.

- Bus, tube, or train. If you can borrow a trolley with wheels from somewhere, this is likely to work better, but you still may have trouble getting heavy things up and into public transport. (Try a cement bag trolley, available online, if you want to invest in your own trolley.)

- Taxis are practical for occasional short journeys. Also the taxi driver may help you get things in and out (tip well if they do!).

- Smartcar or another similar system. If you belong to one of these car share schemes, then you can hire a car fairly cheaply for an hour or two at a time.

- Bike trailer. This is my favourite option. Bike trailers are fabulously useful, environmentally sound, and well worth investing in. They are quite expensive in terms of the initial expenditure, but they should last indefinitely. Cargo bikes are also a similarly useful option.

Bear in mind that if you go by taxi or smartcar, you'll still have to get the stuff from the kerb into your house or flat. Recruit a friend if necessary / possible; or again borrow some kind of trolley or wheely thing. For short journeys, if it's something too large or oddly shaped to be strapped to a bike that's going to be ridden on the road, you may instead be able to balance it on the rack or top tube, keep it steady with one hand, and push the bike along the pavement. Prams and buggies (your own or borrowed) can also be used for transport (they carry more without a child in them), or wheelbarrows if you know someone with a garden or allotment. If you need to borrow something from a friend, try offering them recompense in the form of a share of your crop once you've grown it!

Temperature Zones

This book is oriented to cool temperate climates like the UK and in particular, if I'm discussing my own space, I'm talking about London (which is not only in the south, but also has its own microclimate a couple of degrees warmer than everywhere around it). I've indicated in the text where timings may vary with your local climate.

One of the important dates to be aware of is your local last frost date: you should be wary of planting out anything that isn't cold hardy before this. There are various sites online which will give you this information for your local area.

One measure often used to describing the gardening climate of an area is its Hardiness Zone (a measure invented by the US Department of Agriculture). This categorises areas based on their average winter minimum temperature, and thus categorises plants based on whether they are hardy to that area (will survive that minimum temperature). The table of temperatures is below. London is zone 9 (i.e. minimum temperatures are on average between -1 and -7°C), with most of the rest of the UK being zone 8. A few higher altitude areas (the Highlands and Scottish Uplands, the Pennines, and the top of Snowdonia) are zone 7, and most of coastal Ireland, the whole west coast of England, Scotland, and Wales, and a tiny bit of the east coast of Scotland and north-east England is zone 9 (the North Sea raises the temperature for 5km inland).

If you live outside the UK, your local climate may be in a slightly different zone – again, you can check this out online and make adjustments accordingly. In zones 9-10 (and with some adjustments for frost dates, zone 8) the advice here should still be approximately correct. Unfortunately, if you're living in a tropical area or much further north, you'll probably need to find other sources of information about suitable plants for your climate.

The problem with the hardiness measure is that it only takes into account winter minimum temperatures, not summer maximum temp-

Hardiness Zones		Heat Zones	
Zone	*Minimum temp (°C)*	*Zone*	*Days above 30°C*
1	-51 – -45	1	<1
2	-45 – -40	2	1–7
3	-40 – -35	3	8–14
4	-35 – -29	4	15–30
5	-29 – -23	5	31–45
6	-23 – -17	6	46–90
7	-17 – -12	7	61–90
8	-12 – -7	8	91–120
9	-7 – -1	9	121–150
10	-1 – 4	10	151–180
11	4 – 10	11	181–210
		12	>210

Check Wikipedia for a list of European cities with their hardiness zones: http://en.wikipedia.org/wiki/Hardiness_zone

eratures. The latter obviously have a massive impact on what plants you can successfully grow during your summer. There is also a heat zones map available, based on how many days of the year are above 30°C.

The Wikipedia page referenced above also gives heat zones for some European cities. London is in heat zone 2, as is most of the rest of southern England. The rest of the UK is in heat zone 1. Note that these figures may be changing as the climate changes – make your own observations of your space over time. In particular, as discussed earlier in this chapter, you may have your own microclimate in your space which will affect what you can successfully grow.

The further away your area is from hardiness zone 8-9 and heat zone 1-3, the more you are likely to have to adapt the instructions in this book. It should be adaptable for most temperate climates, but if you're gardening in a tropical or subtropical climate (or a subarctic one!) you'll probably want different information and will be growing different plants.

I should also note that while this book is organised month-by-month, that is based on a northern hemisphere set of seasons. If you're in the southern hemisphere, read January as July, February as August, and so on (so your spring, in October-November, corresponds to April-May in the northern hemisphere). However, you'll still need to take frost dates, hardiness zone, and heat zone into account to adapt the information provided for your own area (in Melbourne, for example, raspberries are a winter crop as it gets too hot in the summer).

CHAPTER 1 | NOVEMBER

By November in the UK, the weather is usually deteriorating noticeably, although there's still hope for some nice bright days. November for the year of this project began for me with a torrential downpour and gales; however, I did manage a quick overview of how things stood.

· ·

My Balcony at the Start of November

Plants still alive and growing:

Herbs: rosemary, thyme, bay, oregano, chives, and parsley (both flat and curly). All but the rosemary and thyme were in the cold frame (see p.36 for how to build yourself a cold frame). I also had one basil plant which I'd moved inside onto a windowsill.

Half a dozen **tomato** plants, still with a handful of unripe tomatoes on.

Salad vegetables on the railing: sorrel, bronze arrowhead lettuce, rocket.

Salad vegetables in the other cold frame: bronze arrowhead lettuce, rocket.

Some slightly pathetic-looking **pak choi**.

Seeds and cuttings:

Several pots with **broad bean** and **pea seeds** in. No sign yet of life.

Four sprigs of **mint**, cuttings taken in late October; as yet unclear if they were going to live or die (but mint is quite tough).

Miscellaneous other:

Possibly some volunteer **potatoes** hiding in the really big pot.

Stacks of empty or half-full **pots** that badly needed to be tidied up.

A black plastic sack of leaves, busily turning themselves into **leafmould**.

The **shed** (been on the 'to-be-deconstructed' list for at least two years, currently full of random bits of wood rescued from skips across London).

Wormery, empty at the start of the month.

The plastic tub of kitchen scraps to go down to the allotment **compost** bin.

Things to Do in November

- Sow beans and peas for overwintering (p.32).

- Tidy up your space (p.176).

- Collect leaves from local parks for leafmould (p.35).

- Move winter herbs and salad veg into a cold frame (p.36 and 39).

- Preserve any green tomatoes still hanging around on the plants, if you haven't already given up on them (p.36).

- Start thinking about and planning next season (p.58).

Beans and Peas

Broad beans and early peas can both be overwintered: this means that you start growing them in October or November, in order to give them a head start in the spring. They won't do much during the winter itself, and that's fine – just keep them watered and wait till it starts getting warmer. You should expect to see a little growth, but you don't want too much, or they'll be more susceptible to frost.

In particular, if you have an aphid problem (which I do on the allotment, and to a lesser extent on the balcony), broad beans are particularly prone to infestation, and in previous years I've lost a whole crop. If you overwinter your plants, you can get them cropping before the aphids really wake up from the winter. You won't get quite as good a crop as you might without the aphid problem, since eventually the aphids will catch up and you likely won't get the later beans; but you'll get enough to be worthwhile. See p.82 for notes on planting out the seedlings in the spring (and p.131 for more on aphids).

Beans and peas sown in the spring are a good candidate for succession sowing; this is when you sow a handful of seeds at weekly or fortnightly intervals, so they'll be at slightly different stages of development and you can extend the cropping season (see p.70 for more). This isn't much use for overwintered plants, though, since the plants tend to catch up with one another while they're growing very slowly over the winter. However, it may be worth staggering your sowing a little bit in case of other accidents (marauding squirrels, for example!).

If you have anywhere else to sow beans or peas (an allotment, or a patch of spare ground somewhere, see p.135 for more on guerrilla gardening), then a few extra baby plants can be useful, too. Beans and peas are pleasingly easy to care for, so they're a good choice for extra or unexpected spaces. See the March chapter for more on increasing your crop and harvesting.

Compost and Leafmould

Compost is incredibly valuable to a gardener, but if you've got a limited space, especially one which is on hard standing, the traditional compost pile won't work well. If you've got enough space, you can set up a rotating-style bin and import some worms into it (much as with a wormery), but even with only a small amount of space, a wormery is well worth the effort of setting it up. Wormeries should be fairly odour-free, so you can even keep them inside if you have a suitable cupboard. See p.22 in the Introduction for more on using your compost in your pots and suitable compost mixes.

Setting up a wormery

I got my wormery subsidised by my local council (Southwark) a couple of years ago. Lots of councils do this, so it's worth investigating. Unfortunately on my first attempt at worm farming, the worms died. This time around, I got a bigger batch of worms (0.5kg instead of 0.25kg, ordered from www. bucketofworms.co.uk) and was determined to pay closer attention to what was going on in there.

My subsidised wormery.

The worms arrived looking incredibly healthy, so I damped down the existing coir bedding a bit, tipped them and their surrounding compost on top of it, and added a small amount of food scraps from our compost collection bucket. Then I topped it with a layer of cardboard, put the lid back on, and left them alone for a few days.

A happy worm on a bed of shredded paper (there were kitchen scraps underneath).

Worms take a while to settle in, and you don't want to overfeed them while they're doing it. Just ignore them while they find their lack of feet. After 2-4 weeks, you can start feeding them a little at a time. Keep an eye on how much of the food scraps are being eaten, and don't feed the worms more than they can handle. As they settle in (and breed!) they'll eat faster. Bear in mind that they also take longer to process food in the winter, as they'll slow down in the colder weather.

Tips for Good Wormcare

- Make sure you have enough worms to get going with initially.

- Do not add citrus (oranges, lemons, and limes) and alliums (onion, garlic, chives); worms can be picky about both.

- If it gets really cold, you may need to wrap your wormery in bubblewrap; but in general worms deal fairly well with cold as long as they've got bedding and food to burrow into. They'll eat a little more slowly, though.

- If it's hot, you may need to move the wormery into the shade.

- Food scraps should be chopped up a little to help the worms chomp through them.

- Use only raw veg scraps, a little paper, and other such things to feed the worms.

No dairy, cooked foods or meat!

- Your wormery should come with a tap so that you can drain off any excess liquid. Make sure you do this regularly so that the worms don't drown.

✳ *Making leafmould*

Leafmould is what happens when autumn leaves rot down. It becomes a crumbly material that's good to use in potting mixes, and can improve your soil. Potting compost used more than once tends to dry out and become dusty, losing a lot of its goodness. Before you replant in the spring, you can tip out the old compost into a bag or container, mix it up a bit with leafmould and compost, and reuse it (see the March chapter for more on this).

The bad news about leafmould is that it takes at least a year to make, so the leaves you collect this autumn won't be usable until the spring after next. But the time will pass whatever you do, so you might as well get on with it now!

Leafmould is incredibly easy to make. Gather up fallen leaves (from deciduous trees – those that lose their leaves in the autumn – not ever-green ones, which take much longer to rot). Stick the leaves in a black plastic bag, and water them a little bit if they're dry, to encourage the rotting process. Poke a few holes in the sides of the bag, tie it loosely shut, and leave it for a year or so. Be aware that waxier leaves, such as plane tree leaves (which is what I have most of locally, unfortunately) may take longer than other types to rot; you may have to leave them for two rather than just one year. If you want to get a bit fancier, and you have the room, you can buy or make wire mesh containers. The advantage of black plastic sacks is that they're more moveable, although they too can rot a bit and be prone to developing holes. Heavy duty bags may be a better bet than the regular dustbin liners.

Leafmould in a black plastic sack.

You can pick up fallen leaves more or less anywhere in the autumn. Local parks are one of the best places; you can also pick up leaves from pavements, but avoid roads as the leaves may have picked up too much in the way of pollutants. Also avoid disturbing drifts of leaves in corners or under hedges, as wildlife may use them to hibernate in. Stick to the huge piles of leaves out in the open under trees. We have a dog, so for a couple of weeks I stuck a plastic carrier bag in my pocket and spent a couple of minutes filling it every time I took the dog to the park, then emptied it into a black plastic sack on the balcony on my return. As I'm terribly lazy, this worked better for me than doing it all at once.

Leafmould is free and easy to make, and it saves the council the energy of taking dead leaves away and doing whatever it is that they do with them, so it's an excellent permaculture option.

If your leaves are rotting too slowly, or if you're otherwise impatient, another option is to use a layer or two of leaves to pad out compost when filling a new container. This should be a largeish container or raised bed, though, rather than a small pot, to be worth doing.

Green Tomatoes

You may find that as the weather starts getting colder, and the tomato plants start looking steadily more pathetic, that you still have a few green tomatoes left on the plants. By November, you need to harvest them anyway, as they're certainly not going to ripen on their own now. Really, you could conclude this a little earlier, but I'm a hopeless optimist; and in sunny autumns have been harvesting fresh tomatoes from a south-facing wall until early November. Tomatoes will sometimes ripen on a window ledge, especially if you put them next to a banana (bananas give off a strong concentration of ethylene gas, which is absorbed by other fruit around them and which encourages ripening). Or you can make green tomato chutney, which is my preference.

Building a Cold Frame

A cold frame is basically a very small, unheated greenhouse. It's a way of providing your plants with a little protection and warmth over the winter: the see-through top lets in the sun, but the enclosed box keeps the plants a little warmer. It also means that you need to water less often, as any water which evaporates will condense on the lid and drop back down onto the plants.

You can buy commercial cold frames, but they're very easy to make with reclaimed bits of wood.

For your base, you can either use an existing wooden box (one of my cold frames uses a wooden wine box that I got from my parents, see p. 178; or sometimes you may find old drawers in skips), or nail together planks. Old pallets are a good source of planks, or again, you can check out nearby skips, or watch for your neighbours doing redecorating work.

Use the planks to create a couple of open rectangles, the same size. You're going to stack these up on top of each other to make the cold frame big enough for the height of your plants. The advantage of making 'rounds' like this is that you can start the cold frame off quite short, and add further rounds as the plants get taller.

You'll also need one round, to sit on the top, which creates a slope, so the cold frame will catch the sun better. It'll work without this, but it's slightly more efficient and effective with it.

Cut the front plank lengthways to leave it a little less than half its previous width. The back one will remain the same. Measure the width

Green Tomato Chutney

This quantity will produce a kilo or so of chutney:

> 500g green tomatoes
> 250g onion (one small onion = 70g)
> 250g apple
> 125g raisins
> 250g brown sugar
> a lump of ginger, finely diced
> a couple of chillies, finely diced
> pinch of salt
> 250ml malt vinegar

OR (alternative version for calculating weights given your own quantity of produce):

> green tomatoes
> half the tomato-weight of onions
> half the tomato-weight of apples
> quarter of the tomato-weight of raisins
> half the tomato-weight of brown sugar
> a lump of ginger, finely diced
> a couple of chillies, finely diced
> pinch of salt
> half the tomato-weight of malt vinegar

Dice the veg fairly finely – but remember, it's basically savoury jam. You needn't worry too much about how neat the chopping is.

Throw everything in a thick bottomed pan, bring to the boil, and stir while the sugar dissolves.

Simmer for at least an hour, until it is jam-like in consistency.

Meanwhile, THOROUGHLY wash enough old jam jars to hold the chutney, and stick them in the oven briefly at 100°C to dry them off and make sure that they're sterilised.

Once the chutney is done, ladle it into the jars (be careful! the glass will be very hot) right up to the top, cover with clingfilm or a jam jar cover, and put the lid on tightly. Leave to cool thoroughly. It can be kept in a cool place until you open it, after which it should stay in the fridge. It will benefit from being left for at least a couple of months before opening, to mellow a little.

This recipe makes reasonably spicy chutney; some people might want less chilli than this. Alternatively, you can chop the chilli and ginger a little larger, and use a bit of muslin or a teaball to hang it in the chutney and pull it out when cooked.

How to make a simple cold frame

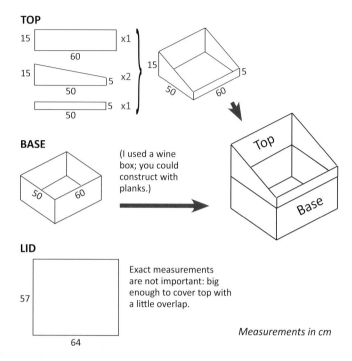

TOP

15 | 60 | x1

15 | 50 | 5 | x2

5 | 50 | x1

15 | 50 | 60 | 5

BASE

50 | 60

(I used a wine box; you could construct with planks.)

Top

Base

LID

57 | 64

Exact measurements are not important: big enough to cover top with a little overlap.

Measurements in cm

of the front plank, mark it on one end of each side plank, and, again on each side plank, draw a diagonal line from the back edge to your mark on the front. Saw along this line, so you end up with two sloped sides. Nail all four planks together.

The final stage is to create a top for it. The classic cold frame top is an old wooden window; again, keep an eye on the local skips (see p.187 for more on skip diving). I managed to get hold of a couple of very large bits of transparent plastic, which I cut to size. If you're using cut plastic or glass, gaffer tape the edges to avoid injury. Again, you can also of course buy something transparent for the top. Plastic sheeting may also work, but it's likely to degrade over time; glass is the longest lasting material.

You can either just balance the top on the cold frame base (my personal preference!), or make hinges (this looks a bit better, and will also avoid potential storm damage if your area isn't sheltered). You'll need to prop the top open a little, to allow air into the box. Also bear in mind that if you're using a wooden box with a base (rather than just making a frame with no base), you should line the bottom with a bit of plastic to catch any water which might drip when you water the plants. An old compost bag is ideal.

Another way of getting a similar effect for a single plant is to chop the top off a plastic bottle (at least 1 litre size, and 2-3l bottles may be better) and place that over the plant with the lid off. You can also make cloches from old bits of glass, but those are better suited for larger beds.

Growing Winter Herbs

Some herbs simply won't grow in the UK over the winter: basil is an example (although you may be able to overwinter it if you bring it inside and coddle it a little, see p.44), and chives will survive and return exuberantly in the spring, but won't actually grow, even in a cold frame. However, quite a few herbs can be kept going, especially if you have access to a cold frame as above.

Rosemary (see p.67) is cold-hardy, and will do fine even out of a cold frame. You should be able to crop a little from it if it's a well-established plant, but be careful not to overdo it. It's unlikely to put much new growth on unless the winter is quite mild, but taking some of the old growth is fine. Good for roast potatoes!

Mint and **parsley** are both cold-hardy, and parsley in particular will keep growing even through a little snow! It's slow growth, though, and you won't be able to use that much of it unless you have a lot of plants. If you're keen to keep it cropping, it's probably worth moving it into a cold frame to encourage more growth, especially if you're a bit further north. Happily, parsley self-seeds with abandon, so after a season or two you may well have plenty of small plants in the corners of pots, and perhaps not even be all that bothered if you accidentally kill off a couple by over-harvesting.

Bay trees are cold-hardy, but like rosemary, there's a limit to how much you can crop over the winter as the plant won't be growing very much if at all.

Sage (see p.42) and thyme (see p.52) will survive without any protection over the winter, but you probably won't be able to crop any of them unless the winter is unusually mild. They're unlikely to put on much new growth and you don't want to chop off all of the old growth for cooking or you'll take away all the plant's reserves. All of these will do well in a cold frame and should grow at least a handful of fresh leaves, in which case you should be able to keep getting (limited!) quantities of fresh herbs from them over the winter.

Oregano (see p.102) will die back altogether over winter, and even in a cold frame may not put on any new growth (though it's worth a go). However, it will return in the spring unless the winter was unusually cold.

In general, though, bear in mind that the plants won't be doing much in the way of new growth (although especially in a cold frame, you may get a little), so you should be careful when cropping. Don't take so much that the plant can't keep itself alive!

Keeping the more delicate herbs (thyme, oregano, even mint and parsley) in a cold frame will mean that they will pick up again much earlier in the spring than they would if just left outdoors, so it's worth it even if you can't use them very much over the winter. Parsley is biennial: it sets seed in its second year. So a parsley plant will keep going happily for a full year, before flowering and setting seed in the second year, after which it dies. Either save the seeds, or let it sow itself in the surrounding pots.

Bear in mind as well that you can freeze or dry fresh herbs throughout the year to give yourself a supply of your own herbs through the winter months.

Herbs doing well in the cold frame over the winter.

Sage

Growing

Sage can be started from seed, but it grows very slowly, so you'll have a while to wait – usually around 15 months – until you can actually use it. The other alternative is a cutting, which should take about three months to establish itself.

If raising from seed, sow indoors in March, or outdoors in April, and then expect to be able to harvest in June of the next year. When it's grown enough to pot into a larger pot, incorporate plenty of compost or even a little manure into the potting material.

Cuttings should be taken in the spring (5cm long); after three or four years, a plant will start to lose its strength and flavour, so you should expect to repropagate from a cutting of the original plant about every three years. It's fine just to take a cutting from your existing plant: as this grows into a new plant it will become more flavourful again.

Sage needs full sun for at least some of the day, but can tolerate partial shade. A medium soil is best, but in particular it doesn't want soil that is always moist, as it's a Mediterranean plant that is drought tolerant. If you look at the leaves, the velvety texture and their slightly padded feel are adaptations to enable the plant to survive without much water when necessary.

Sage likes a little fertiliser a couple of times per summer, and should be pruned back after the flowers die down. It grows very well in a pot.

Culinary uses

Sage is often used to season meat or poultry. It's good in sausages, and is also often used in stuffing (which can be vegetarian). For vegetarians, it's good in soups or stews, especially ones with beans or lentils in them, and goes particularly well with squash dishes. It's best used fresh, but sage leaves keep well in the freezer, and you can also dry it for later use by hanging it in a warm, dry place.

It also goes well with cheese, and baked into biscuits.

Be warned: the flavour is quite strong, so use sage sparingly.

Medicinal uses

Sage tea is good for respiratory infection, nasal congestion, coughs, tonsillitis and sore throats. To prepare, pour boiling water over 1-2 teaspoons of sage leaves, cover, and leave to infuse for ten minutes. Drink one or two cups per day.

Sage tea can also be helpful if you're suffering from indigestion, and is said to be good for the liver. And it tastes lovely, so you can just drink it for pleasure!

Mixing a little crushed sage with your toothpaste can help to remove plaque and strengthen the gums, as it has an antiseptic effect.

Some studies have shown that sage can improve memory function. There is also some evidence that sage can inhibit the enzyme acetylcholinesterase (AChE); deficiency in AChE is associated with Alzheimer's. Research is currently underway to investigate whether sage can help people with Alzheimer's. Sage is known to be well-tolerated, with few side effects, so this is very promising research if it proves to be effective. Meanwhile, increasing the amount of sage in your diet is hardly a hardship!

CHAPTER 2

DECEMBER

By December it's definitely cold enough that you need to start thinking about protecting delicate plants. In more northerly areas, or if you get an early frost in southern areas, you might need to do this earlier – keep an eye on the weather forecast if you have very delicate plants such as citrus trees (see p.65). There's not that much growing, but any autumn greens you sowed in October should be producing, as should some hardy herbs and lettuces. There's also chickweed if you care to try a bit of urban foraging! And, of course, the end of December means Christmas, when you may be able to use a few herbs from your pots.

My Balcony at the Start of December

Plants still alive and growing:

    Herbs: rosemary, thyme, bay, oregano, chives, and parsley (both flat and curly). All but the rosemary and thyme are in a cold frame (see p.36). One basil plant surviving on an inside windowsill.

    Salad vegetables on the railing: sorrel, bronze arrowhead lettuce, rocket.

    Salad vegetables in the smaller cold frame: bronze arrowhead lettuce, rocket.

    Some slightly pathetic-looking **pak choi**.

Seeds and cuttings:

    Several pots with **broad bean** and **pea seeds** in. Still no sign of life.

    Four sprigs of **mint**, planted in late October; two looking healthy, two less healthy.

Miscellaneous other:

    Pots all tidied up and last year's plants put in the compost.

Things to Do in December

- **Protect** delicate plants from the cold (p.44).
- Forage for **chickweed** (p.47).

Protecting Plants from the Cold

By December in the UK, there's not that much daylight (and what there is fairly weak), and it's getting pretty cold. Most of your annuals will have had it by now, and if you haven't taken cold-sensitive plants (such as basil) inside already it may be too late.

Basil, like other cold-sensitive herbs, will live through the winter on an inside windowsill, but it won't look very happy, and you won't get much

Basil flowering on my windowsill in the winter.

(if any) basil for cooking over the winter. The aim is just to keep it alive until the weather warms up again, when you may get a few more leaves before it goes to seed, while you're waiting for the spring sowing to get going. The same is true for other cold-sensitive plants, which are often grown as annuals in the UK, such as peppers. In theory, some of these plants can be grown as perennials, if you keep them warm enough. You're unlikely to get even leafy plants to crop (obviously fruit bearing plants will not produce fruit until the next flowering season), but if you can keep them alive, they'll get going faster in the spring than if you have to restart from seed. I've been able to keep pepper and chilli plants alive over the winter this way, and got a head start on fruiting the next season as a result.

Some cold-sensitive plants that are too large to move indoors can still be nursed through the winter if you're lucky and take a few precautions, particularly if your space is south-facing and/or sheltered. For some plants, a cold frame (see p.36) may be sufficient. For plants too large for a cold frame, or which need more protection than that, you'll need to apply further insulation to help them make it through the cold weather.

When you grow a plant in the ground, rather than in a pot, its roots are underground, surrounded by a lot of earth in all but one direction (upwards), and able to burrow downwards away from the surface if need be. Earth holds heat reasonably well, and the upper layers of earth insulate the lower layers. Over the course of a long cold winter, the earth will slowly freeze from the surface downwards, but in the southern UK cold spells rarely last long enough for this to be very deep. Even in the northern UK (except in the very highest parts), ground frost averages only 17-19 days in December and January, meaning that frost won't penetrate too deeply. So for a plant which is rooted in the ground, the earth itself will protect the plant's roots, and the plant can root itself as deeply as it needs (within its own limitations). In a pot, there's no such protection, and the roots can't go anywhere to get away from the cold. So the first step is to insulate the pot.

Put your delicate plant in the warmest and sunniest corner you have, then wrap its pot in bubblewrap (or garden fleece if you don't mind spending the money on it), and cover the earth around the plant with fabric underneath a layer of insulation (more bubblewrap or fleece). Make sure that the fabric is gathered up around the trunk of the plant, between the trunk and the insulating material. This prevents moisture from collecting around the trunk of the plant when you water, potentially rotting it. You can also put a little gravel around the trunk of the plant to protect it further.

It's important to make sure that the drainage of the pot is good, to avoid roots rotting (good drainage is of course important at any time of year, but you can get away with poor drainage when it's hot where you can't when it's cold), and water minimally over the winter. Drainage and moisture issues are less of a problem if you have an area (as I do) where rain won't fall on the pots.

The trunk of tree-like plants may also need to be protected if it's going to be really cold. You can use bubblewrap for this as well, but, again, you need to use a fabric wrap underneath, to avoid moisture collecting underneath the plastic. Alternatively, you can use straw and chicken wire. Push the chicken wire into the pot about 5cm from the trunk all around, then fill the gap tightly with straw. You can do a similar thing on the cheap with a cardboard box taped into a tube and leaves or straw (or even shredded paper) packed around the trunk. Using straw or paper like this means that the wrapping is breathable as well as protective, which avoids potential moisture problems. You can also get commercial products to do the same job.

Some even more delicate plants may benefit from having the whole plant, up to the crown, insulated. This will depend on how cold your particular microclimate gets (see p.11 for a further discussion of microclimates), and how robust the plant is. You can use exactly the same techniques to protect as much of the plant as you want.

I have a satsuma tree which isn't cold-hardy, and got it through a winter with several snowfalls by wrapping pot, earth, and trunk in bubblewrap; so this technique can be very successful.

Plants that don't need cold protection

Of course, not all plants are cold-sensitive. In southern England, rocket, lettuce and sorrel all have a good chance of coping with cold weather, and may even keep growing. The rocket and bronze arrowhead lettuce on the edge of my balcony kept on growing sufficiently for me to harvest leaves, albeit only a few, right through a fortnight of snow. Chard and kale are both cold-hardy too, although chard leaves can get a little tough in the winter.

As discussed in the previous chapter, rosemary, sage, thyme, parsley, oregano, and chives will all survive the winter, as will bay trees, although you may not be able to crop all of them throughout the season (see p.39 for more details). A cold frame will help maximise your winter herb production.

Overwintered rocket and bronze arrowhead lettuce in an outside trough in February, still looking very healthy.

Even for the plants that are happy outside a cold frame, if you have space to move them into one, you're much more likely to get some new growth (slower than in the summer, but still there) through the winter. However, you still need to be careful about how much you take at any one time. Keep an eye on how the plant is doing, and take a little at a time. Similarly, lettuce and rocket will do well in a cold frame and will grow more prolifically than their unprotected counterparts.

The best bet, really (and this is something I will be saying throughout this book) is to experiment. Leave one of your parsley seedlings outside, put the other in the cold frame. (If you only have one parsley plant right now, don't worry; wait till it seeds itself next year and you'll have thousands of them.) See which one does best, or if there's an important difference at all. The same approach is good with other plants, too. Check whether it needs protecting to survive the winter at all, and then see where it does best. Make sure you keep some kind of record somewhere, or you'll have to do it all over again the next year. This approach helps you to get to know how your own space works and what is the best thing for you to do in **your** conditions. I can make recommendations here, but all spaces and locations are different (as discussed on p.8), and the best way to make the most of your space is to try things out and see what works and what doesn't work.

The most important point for all your plants is: don't forget to water them. They won't need too much water when it's cold (so check the soil surface and don't over-water either), but if forgotten entirely they will dry out and die. (This has happened to me, one winter when I was away and no one else remembered to water anything.) One advantage of having lettuce and rocket growing through the winter is that you'll be reminded to water when you go out to pick some to eat. If your space is open to rain then you are much less likely to need to worry about this, but with the odd weather we've had over the last few years, you may get surprisingly dry spells in October or November.

Foraging

Chickweed

One of the approaches that permaculture teaches is to consider other spaces around you and how they can be productive. I'll talk about foraging in various places in this book, and there's more discussion of it on p.183.

Chickweed is a godsend in winter, and you'll almost certainly be able to locate some. It's an excellent source of vitamins A, C, D, and B complex, as well as minerals including iron, calcium, potassium, and zinc. It's nice raw, as a salad leaf, or you can cook it in the same way that you would a spinach.

It's a very prolific weed that you'll find in neglected flower beds, on vacant lots, on grass, and possibly in parks. It grows in

Chickweed growing on the grass near my flat in January.

open areas, but also does well in partially shaded ones, such as at the base of trees, and does best anywhere that's cool and damp. As with most weed species, it thrives on disturbed soil. It may even establish itself in your own pots and containers. While it grows all year round, it does best when other, taller, plants aren't shading it out altogether – which tends to mean in late autumn and early spring, and during the winter when it's not actually snowing. It grows right through the winter – I harvested chickweed in January when writing this book.

It can be identified by its very low, branching habit, and by its leaves, which grow in opposed pairs, with a length of bare stalk between each pair of leaves. If it's flowering, you'll see tiny white flowers right at the top. When harvesting, snip off the leafy tops and leave the lower stalks, which get a bit tough. The harvesting will encourage more growth, so you can come back in a bit to get another harvest. Definitely avoid pulling it up by the roots, or you won't be able to come back for more another time. And as always, never take so much that you damage the plant.

Be aware that chickweed picked from public spaces will definitely need to be washed, and consider the likely paths of both animals and humans across the area you're picking from. Avoid picking wild plants from next to busy roads, as they'll have soaked up plenty of pollution.

Eating chickweed

Chickweed is nice as a green salad leaf, with a very clean, 'green' taste. Add it to your cultivated winter lettuce and rocket salads. You can also cook it like spinach (perhaps with dandelion leaves, when it comes to the spring; winter dandelion leaves are too tough to be worth eating, although now is a great time to harvest dandelion roots, as on p.180).

I made a very nice vegan chickweed pesto recipe this year. If you're not vegan, you could put a decent-size lump of Parmesan cheese in to replace the nutritional yeast.

I found that this worked well on pasta, but I also enjoyed it on crackers for the next few days as a mid-morning snack.

Medicinal value

Chickweed is very high in a number of minerals (including copper, iron, magnesium, zinc, and calcium), and is an excellent source of Vitamin C. A serving of chickweed may be a good option if you think you're about to come down with a cold.

VEGAN CHICKWEED PESTO

Ingredients:

A few good handfuls of chickweed tops (I had maybe a couple of packed mugs' worth).

Handful of pine nuts or sunflower seeds.

1 or 2 cloves raw garlic (if you can leave the pesto overnight to mellow), or 2 teaspoons minced garlic/ garlic paste (if you want to eat it immediately).

Tablespoon nutritional yeast (use Parmesan for a non-vegan pesto).

Generous pinch of salt.

2-3 tablespoons olive oil (add as needed while blending).

Throw all the ingredients into a blender and keep blending until it looks like pesto. Add the olive oil as needed to help the blender out (you can also add a very little water), and as needed for texture.

You can dry it (wash and spread out somewhere warm) and make an infusion from it, which is supposed to be good for coughs and hoarseness. Pour boiling water over a small handful of dried chickweed, cover, and leave for 10-30 minutes. Strain before drinking. I found that it didn't taste of very much, although it had a slightly sweet aftertaste; and I wasn't convinced about the soothing effect, either. (I'd rather drink thyme tea (p.53) for a sore throat or a cough, myself.) The tea is also a mild diuretic and is supposed to cleanse the kidneys, and may be helpful if you're suffering from cystitis. Used externally as a wash, the tea may help soothe skin irritation.

You can also macerate chickweed in oil to use as a healing oil for minor skin irritation. It must be dried thoroughly first, otherwise dangerous bacteria can grow in the oil from the damp parts. As above, to dry, spread it on a tea-towel and leave it somewhere warm. Once dry, put it in a jar and pour oil over it, then label it and leave it in the sun for a couple of weeks. Move it to a dark cupboard after that, and use to treat minor skin issues topically as necessary. Do not take internally.

It is suggested that chickweed should be avoided if pregnant or breastfeeding; this seems to be because the effects haven't been studied rather than because of any documented problems. If eating in moderation, you are likely to be fine, but I would recommend doing your own research and consulting a doctor if in doubt. Very excessive consumption of chickweed *may* cause nitrate poisoning (one case, and the conclusion is controversial), but eating it in moderation as a vegetable is very unlikely to cause problems.

Food from Your Balcony for Christmas Dinner

So, what can you eat from your balcony for Christmas dinner? It's possible to get a handful of potatoes, if you sowed at the right time of year (about 16 weeks previously, so in August, see p.161) and have a really big pot or a thick plastic sack (see p.97 for how to sow potatoes). You're very unlikely to get enough to satisfy the family appetite for roast potatoes, unfortunately!

What you can quite easily get is a few sprigs of fresh rosemary to roast your bought potatoes with; and a bay leaf for the gravy. Sage and onion stuffing is another popular Christmas dinner option, and fresh sage should be available if you have a well-established plant, or if you have a smaller plant but have put it in a cold frame. Parsley is cold-hardy and is nice with parsnips or in a lentil loaf or vegetable stuffing.

You can also make up a small but very tasty fresh salad from what-ever rocket and lettuce leaves are still on the go. Eating fresh salad leaves directly from your own little patch in the middle of December is a wonderful treat. It's also nice for a stomach that is feeling a little over-abused.

Medicinal Herbs for the Party Season

If you're suffering from overindulgence (in either food or drink), your balcony herbs may be able to help.

For an upset stomach or to settle nausea, try a few leaves of peppermint (p.162) steeped in boiling water. Peppermint is well-known for its digestive properties, and also contains antioxidants, which can help to prevent other forms of alcohol damage. Ginger (p.181) is another herb which is great for soothing the stomach. Suck on a little raw ginger root, or steep some grated ginger root in boiling water.

A few leaves of fresh or dried thyme (p.52) in water can help relax tired or stressed muscles, so may help with a headache. (The water itself will help, too, especially if you add a drop of honey.) Thyme is also good for settling the stomach. Yarrow (p.172), basil (p.144), coriander, and rosemary (p.67) are all herbs which have folk-value as hangover cures (in all cases, steep some of the herb in boiling water, and drink with a little honey to taste), although in reality it may just be the water that does the work. Whatever else you do, make sure to drink plenty of water as well to help your body deal with the excess food or booze you put into it. Then go have a nap on the sofa to recover.

Thyme

Thyme is a perennial herb which will survive the winter even unprotected. However, it will do better in a cold frame, in which case you may get some fresh growth and be able to harvest a little more from it over the cold season.

There are many types of thyme. *Thymus vulgaris* (also known as English thyme or French thyme; but check the Latin name if buying in a garden centre, as the common names sometimes apply to other species) is the best variety for cooking and the most commonly used one. Lemon thyme (*Thymus x citriodorus* – again, check the Latin name if buying) smells lovely, but the citrus scent doesn't really survive cooking, so in limited space it may not be worth it.

Growing

Thyme can be grown from seed: sow in spring, with a very little soil covering the seeds, and keep the soil damp but not wet until the seedlings are big enough to plant on into a bigger pot (after they have a couple of sets of real leaves).

You can also grow thyme from cuttings, if you have access to another plant. Take older stems, cut them diagonally with a sharp knife to give a clean cut, and strip the leaves from the lower part of the stem. The usual recommendation is to cut just above the woody part, but I've had success with woody stems as well. Avoid flowering stems, as they'll be more reluctant to root. Take plenty of cuttings, and stick them all fairly deeply into a light compost mix, then leave somewhere shady, watering regularly. After a few weeks, the cuttings should have rooted enough to be potted up, hardened off, and moved outside.

To help cuttings along, you can obtain commercial rooting hormone; alternatively, a more natural (and cheaper) option is to make a willow bark rooting tonic. Willow, after all, is very good at rooting itself.

Take a fresh willow twig, break it into 5cm chunks, put it in a bowl, and cover it with boiling water. Leave overnight for the bark to infuse into the water. Dip your cuttings into this infusion after you've cut them across diagonally and just before you put them into the soil. I also usually water afterwards with a little of the infusion. The infusion will keep in the fridge (label clearly!) for a couple of months.

Thyme likes a reasonably dry soil (so don't over-water, as damp can kill it), and similarly does better on reasonably poor soil. It likes plenty of sun, but it's cold-hardy and will survive the winter (in a sunny place and/or with a cold frame, it may even keep growing). As a spreading plant, it needs horizontal space more than vertical, so it will do well in a wide/long and shallow container.

If possible, put some gravel at the bottom of the pot, and maybe also a shallow layer on the top, to reduce soil erosion.

Once it's established, you can leave it pretty much to its own devices, and it will grow away happily. It's drought tolerant, but does better when watered intermittently (as above, not too much water). Add a little fertiliser annually, but thyme, like most herbs, doesn't need much.

Trim regularly over spring and summer when you want some thyme for cooking, to keep it bushy, then trim back hard in late summer after flowering to avoid it becoming woody. When trimming, for whatever reason, avoid cutting back into the older (woody) part of the plant, as the green stems tend to grow better. The exception to this is if you're cutting a stem back altogether. You can dry the trimmings and store them for later use. Hang the branches or sprigs somewhere warm, then rub off the leaves and store them in an airtight jar once they're dry.

Culinary uses

Thyme can be used fresh or dry (as above, it's easy to dry, and this is a great way to use any excess trimmings). You should use about a third as much dry herb as you would fresh herb (so one teaspoon of dried thyme is about equal to 1 tablespoon of fresh thyme).

It goes very nicely with tomatoes, and combines well with rosemary, oregano or marjoram, and sage. Thyme keeps its sharp flavour even through long cooking, so it's a good choice for soups or stews. It blends well with onion and garlic-based dishes to make a good savoury stock or a marinade. It's also nice in herb butter.

You can use whole twigs of thyme in the roasting pan when roasting vegetables (or meat), but the twigs themselves will be woody so should be removed before serving. Thyme leaves can be either chopped or used whole (since they're so small). Remove the leaves from the stem by holding the top of the stem and running your other finger and thumb down the stem against the direction of growth.

Medicinal uses

Thyme is a powerful antiseptic and anti-fungal. Thyme infusions (a couple of sprigs of thyme steeped in boiling water for 5 minutes) are good to gargle with for sore throats, coughs, and colds, and can be drunk to settle the stomach. It can also be applied to the skin to soothe skin irritations and infections (most notably athlete's foot). Drinking thyme infusions may also help with Candida infections. Honey is a nice sweetener for thyme tea.

Be aware that essential oil extracted from the thyme plant (not something you'll be doing at home) is very powerful and should not be taken internally. Thyme as an infusion or used as a culinary plant is fine.

CHAPTER 3

JANUARY

January is all about planning for the next season, while it's still cold, dark, and probably damp outside. Getting hold of some seeds now can remind you that spring really is on its way.

· ·

My Balcony at the Start of January

Plants still alive and growing:

Herbs: rosemary, thyme, bay, oregano, chives, and parsley (both flat and curly). One **basil** plant inside on a sunny windowsill.

Salad vegetables on the railing: sorrel, bronze arrowhead lettuce, rocket.

Salad vegetables in the other cold frame: bronze arrowhead lettuce, rocket.

Some slightly pathetic-looking **pak choi**.

Seeds and cuttings:

Several pots with **broad bean and pea seedlings** in. Starting to grow.

Four sprigs of **mint**: two looking healthy, two not.

Green salad veg in the coldframe in January; still cropping nicely.

Things to Do in January

- Acquire seeds (p.56).

- Plan your growing season (p.58).

- Plant rhubarb or berries (pp.62-64).

- Order citrus trees (p.65).

Seeds

Before you can get plants, you're going to need seeds (or in some cases, baby plants or cuttings – see the various individual plant sections for discussion about which method is best for which plant). Seeds are fairly cheap even if you get them all from your nearest garden centre. However, if you want organic seeds or non-hybrid open pollinating seed so that you can seed save (see later on this section for more on this), you may be better off ordering online. See p.192 for a list of suggested organic non-hybrid seed providers.

There are other ways to get hold of seeds rather than buying them, too.

Seed swaps

Seed swaps are where you get together with a bunch of other gardeners, and exchange the seeds that you don't need. This can be particularly useful if you're gardening in a small space, as you'll almost certainly have more seeds in a packet than you want to use. Gardening or allotment clubs or other gardening groups in your area may run seed and plant swaps, or you could get together with any friends who garden. To be even more organised about it, talk to gardening friends before the start of the season, and get a bunch of seed packets to share out between you. You can also get hold of cuttings this way, and if you meet up again in April or May, you may even be able to swap seedlings with one another (it's very common to end up with more seedlings than you really have room for – I end up trying to give away a handful of tomato plants every year).

Seed saving

From your second year onwards, if you want to, you can start saving the seeds from the previous year's plants, and using those for next year. In theory, this means that for any plants suitable for seed saving, you only buy one lot of seeds (your first year), after which you can grow from those plants. This has the advantage of being cheap, but also the advantage that you can do a bit of selection. You can pick the seeds from the plants that have done best (most vigorous, tastiest fruit, highest yield), plant those, and then choose the best ones again next year to save their seed. This way, you gradually breed plants that do particularly well in your own conditions.

Bear in mind that you don't have or need to do this! If you're interested, it can be fun; but there's nothing wrong with getting all of your seeds from shops or from friends. If you're inclined to give it a go, start out with some of the easiest seeds, like tomatoes or rocket.

If you do want to try seed saving, you'll need make sure that the seeds you get in the first place are for plants that will breed true. The vast majority of garden centres sell what are called F1 hybrid seeds. These are a cross between two different and very heavily inbred parent plants, which are bred to produce particular results, often aimed more at large industrial farms than at the home grower. The seed companies are often selecting for uniformity of shape or colour, while most home growers are more interested in taste and suitability for their own specific conditions. In addition to this, the seed produced by F1 plants will usually be sterile (so you can't seed save), or if not sterile won't breed true to the parent. (Which means that the only way to get the same thing again is to buy more seed from the seed company...)

If you want to seed save, then, you need to make sure that you're buying 'real' open-pollinated seed, from someone like the Real Seed Company (see p.192 for suggested seed providers).

Some plants are easier to save seeds from than others are; for example, some plants are quite hard to breed true, especially in a small space. Plants that are air-pollinated can cross with anything within a quarter of a mile; so if you're trying to save chard seed and there's any other chard, beets, or spinach within that distance, your seeds won't breed true, and you'll get something unpredictable (and in most cases, probably less tasty) next year.

Also, some plants are biennial, and only set seed in their second year (this includes carrots). You can lay them aside over the winter, then replant and wait for the seed, but you may decide that it's easier just to buy more seeds next year, especially if your space is limited, as these plants won't provide an actual crop to eat.

If you want to give seed saving a go, there's more information on how to go about it, and selecting the correct plants to save seed from, on pp.90-107 and p.107.

Cuttings

A cutting is a piece taken from an existing plant, which then (given the opportunity) will root and turn into a brand new plant, identical to the old one. Some herbs do very well from cuttings, but most vegetables need to be grown from seed. For all the plants described in this book, I've mentioned if it's possible to grow them from a cutting. It's best to take cuttings in either autumn or spring.

Planning this Season

If this isn't your first year of growing, hopefully you've been able to keep a few hardy green things or some herbs going into January. Even if it is your first year, maybe you've got a tray or two of microgreens on a windowsill by now that are providing you with a few cheering shoots over the darkest part of the year (see p.128, I started a tray of microgreens on New Year's Day this year, though admittedly they grew quite slowly).

If you're starting from scratch right now, while January may not be a good time for most sowing, it's a great time for planning for the start of the growing season. By March you can be starting off seeds, and if you have a sunny windowsill, you may even be thinking about getting a few going in February. So to make the most of your time once spring sidles finally into view, it's good to have everything planned, set up and organised in advance.

If you're just starting out, there's lots of information in the Introduction (p.1) on basic provisions – pots, compost, water, and tools. Now is a good time to start getting hold of the pots and the containers you want, as you've got a couple of months to find the right things, and can avoid spending a fortune because you're buying in a hurry. For compost, you can get a wormery going at any time of year (see p.33), and start making your own free compost from your kitchen scraps. Admittedly this is unlikely to produce all that much over the next couple of months, so you'll need to acquire some from elsewhere anyway (see p.20).

Now is also a good time to acquire seeds, once you've worked out what you want to grow. If you're buying seeds and you leave it too late, you may find that some types of seeds have sold out – particularly if you're interested in rare or unusual varieties, and/or are buying from a small organic supplier like Real Seeds. (See p.192 for a list of seed suppliers).

In addition, if you're ordering online, there'll be a time lag between order and delivery which can be very frustrating when the days are getting longer and you're keen to get going. Starting now also gives you time to find seeds through other means, as discussed in the previous section.

Of course, the first step has to be deciding what you want to grow! Start by thinking about what you most enjoy eating, and what your space is best suited to growing. The sunnier your space, the easier it'll be to grow more or less anything you fancy. Even if you want plants that do better in part-shade, you can create that by stacking plants up and using the shade created by other, taller, plants and pots. (See p.15 for more on using vertical space well.)

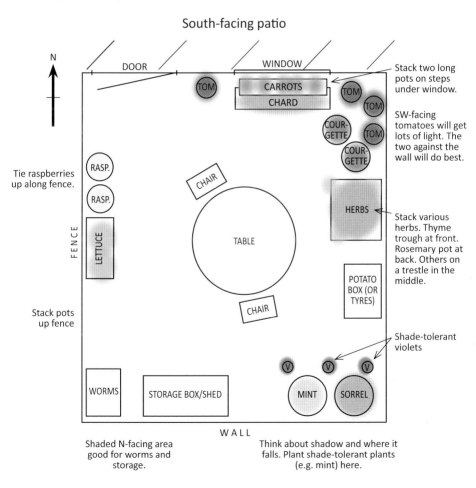

South-facing patio

But even a damp, north-facing space can have promise. Land cress grows well in shade during the summer (less well in winter), and wild garlic (ramsons) also thrives in shade, being a woodland plant. Wood sorrel and the various varieties of mint will all grow in shade. Other options include chard, winter lettuce, mustard greens, alpine strawberries, and autumn raspberries. See p.10 and p.15 for more information on how to plan according to your space.

Now is the time to start making sketches of how you'd like your space to look this year. Your plans may not work out exactly as you intend, of course. Plants have a mind of their own, and accidents happen (sometimes happy ones!). But a good plan gives you a starting point to work from, and something to aim towards.

Once you've decided what you want to grow, it's time to order or otherwise acquire the seeds, and to create a sowing timeline. This should be a note of what you want to sow, where (inside or out?) and when. It doesn't need to be absolutely accurate – 'early April' or 'late February' is good enough. See opposite for an example of mine for one year.

North-facing space outside a front door

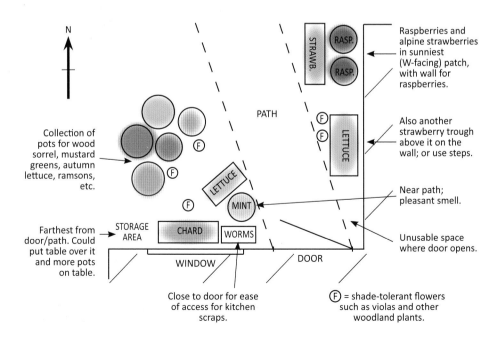

N

RASP.

STRAWB.

RASP.

Raspberries and alpine strawberries in sunniest (W-facing) patch, with wall for raspberries.

PATH

F

F

LETTUCE

Also another strawberry trough above it on the wall; or use steps.

Collection of pots for wood sorrel, mustard greens, autumn lettuce, ramsons, etc.

F

F

LETTUCE

MINT

Near path; pleasant smell.

F

Unusable space where door opens.

Farthest from door/path. Could put table over it and more pots on table.

STORAGE AREA

CHARD

WORMS

WINDOW

DOOR

Close to door for ease of access for kitchen scraps.

(F) = shade-tolerant flowers such as violas and other woodland plants.

West-facing window boxes

1. ANNUAL GREEN LEAVES: replant each year or allow to self-seed.

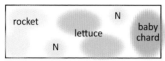

N = nasturtiums to deter aphids

2. Mostly PERENNIAL HERBS.

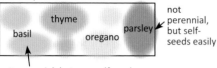

not perennial, but self-seeds easily

not perennial, but may self-seed

3. FRUIT!

also add flowers if you like

Small north-facing space by front door

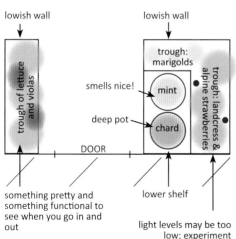

lowish wall

lowish wall

trough: marigolds

trough of lettuce and violas

smells nice!

mint

trough: landcress & alpine strawberries

deep pot

chard

DOOR

something pretty and something functional to see when you go in and out

lower shelf

light levels may be too low; experiment

Sowing Timeline

January
Nothing

February
Early peas

March
Rocket (one early sowing, one late sowing)
Bronze arrowhead lettuce
Parsley
Mangetout
Tomatoes on the windowsill inside
Peppers on the windowsill inside
Thyme on the windowsill inside

April
Rocket (two sowings)
Bronze arrowhead lettuce
Parsley
Carrots (two sowings)
Basil (on windowsill inside)

May
Mizuna
Carrots (two sowings)
Plant out tomatoes
Plant out peppers
Plant out thyme
Courgettes on the windowsill inside
Plant out basil

June
Carrots (two sowings)
Mizuna
Plant out courgettes

July
Mizuna

August
Mizuna
Rocket

September
Mizuna (for overwintering under cover)
Rocket (for overwintering under cover or outside)

Now sit back and relax before the start of the growing season!

Growing Fruit in Pots

It's not just salad vegetables and herbs; even fruit can be grown in pots. Some fruits will do better than others, but here's a run down of a few that may work well. Perennial fruit like raspberries will need a good-sized pot (bigger than you might think for the size of the cane) as they tend to have spreading roots which they need to crop well, but some fruit is also suitable for smaller pots. Even apple or pear trees can be grown in containers, but you will need a suitably large container and a dwarf variety of tree. The barge gardens at Downings Road moorings on the Thames near London Bridge have a variety of trees, including some apples, all growing in 40cm deep containers in the barges – an impressive achievement!

Strawberries

Strawberries are among the easiest fruit to grow in pots. They do well in reasonably small pots or troughs – try a long window box-style container, or one of the hanging strawberry pots you can buy. You could construct your own version from a larger plastic container by cutting some holes in its sides. There's more information on growing strawberries on p.114.

Most strawberries are grown from suckers, in early autumn; but Alpine strawberries can be grown from seed in spring. Alpine strawberries are also tolerant of shady conditions, unlike most regular strawberry varieties which need 6-8 hours of sunshine per day. Note that Alpine strawberries are not a variety of the regular domestic strawberry, but a different plant with much smaller fruit and very different growing conditions. The fruit is tiny, but very tasty and very intensely strawberry-ish.

Different varieties of strawberries also crop at different times: early varieties produce fruit for three weeks around June, and 'everbearing' produce both an early and a late crop. Choose one, or pick two different varieties to extend the season and maximise your crop.

Raspberries and blackberries

Raspberries and blackberries (and assorted crosses like tayberries and loganberries) can be grown in pots, although I admit that I've never had much luck myself in doing this. Other gardeners have, though, so if you like berries, it's worth a go.

Cane fruit like this isn't grown from seed, but from a fruit cane. You can buy these from a shop or an online grower, but they tend to want to sell them in multiples, and you may only want one or two at most. See if you can band together with a friend, or alternatively, if you know anyone who has a garden or allotment with fruit canes, ask them in the autumn if they can spare a cutting. Raspberries spread like mad underground (blackberries do the same, but overground via stolons), and your friend will likely spend a fair amount of time hacking unwanted suckers/stolons out of the ground. They will be happy to rehome one of them with you! Ask your friend to get as much of the root system as possible out of the ground with the sucker, to give it the best chance of surviving once transplanted.

Raspberries come in a multitude of varieties. Autumn Bliss is one good option as it's fairly restrained in terms of foliage, so it won't take over your space too much, and it crops for a very long time. It's an autumn raspberry, so it'll start slightly later than summer raspberries – August or thereabouts – but I've experienced it cropping into November in my allotment, and it'll certainly still be doing well in late September. The fruit are large, and it gives a bigger yield than my earlier raspberries. It's also easier to manage because it fruits on that year's canes, so you just cut it back at the end of the season (see below). If you have a bit more room and can get a couple of single canes, it's a good idea to get one early and one autumn variety, to extend the season as far as possible.

Put the cutting in a pot at least 38cm in diameter, and make sure to provide plenty of food during the growing season, and then to mulch well with fresh compost in March. Water well during dry periods. Use garden canes to train the stems up as they grow, or tie them into points on a wall if growing them up a wall. They're much easier to tie in if you do it little and often, when the canes are still thin.

Other than the annual tying in and cutting back, the plant will mostly look after itself, which is one of the joys of perennial fruit. Provide plenty of water and some food, and let it get on with fruiting. Summer raspberries won't set fruit their first year, as they grow the canes in one year, then set fruit on them the next. Autumn raspberries, or blackberries, ought to give a crop from year one, although it is likely to be a small one initially. Tie the canes back or in as they grow, to avoid them getting out of hand and generating a small jungle on your balcony.

In the autumn, after the fruit has finished (in warmer climes this may not be till November with autumn raspberries, if you're lucky!), cut back the previous year's canes for summer raspberries (i.e. the canes that fruited this year), and all the canes for autumn raspberries. They'll grow more the next year. Blackberries are treated like summer raspberries: cut out the fruit-bearing canes. You should also thin blackberries in early spring, prune side branches to about 30cm, and then tie the canes back. With blackberries in particular, gloves are strongly recommended when pruning!

It is possible to get an early spring crop from autumn raspberries if you leave last year's canes through the winter. Feed the plant well if you're going to do this, so it still has the strength to grow the new canes and fruit on them. Cut the old canes back once they're finished fruiting in the spring/early summer, to give the new ones a bit more space.

Rhubarb

To grow container rhubarb, put a single crown (a section of root) in winter (when the crowns are dormant) into a pot at least 30cm in diameter. It may well do better in a 38cm or even 45cm pot if you have the space. You may be able to get a crown from a friend who's dividing theirs in the winter (see below), or you can buy online or from a garden centre.

Once it's planted, avoid disturbing it for at least 3-5 years. It likes full sun, and well-drained moist soil. Always water at the base of the plant to avoid the stems rotting or rusting. Apply fertiliser a couple of times during the growing season. It's very frost tolerant; and indeed, is incredibly tough and long-lived in general.

Do not harvest in the first year – the plant needs time to get established. Just leave it and let the leaves die back in the autumn. To harvest once the plant is old enough, simply twist the stems away at the base of the plant. Leave 3 or 4 stalks on the plant to feed it for next year. Twist off the leaf (it makes good compost!), and cook the stem. Rhubarb crumble is one traditional cooking option, and stewed rhubarb is also nice. Rhubarb and ginger jam will preserve it if you have too much.

After a few years (possibly as many as ten), the plants will start to decrease in vigour. At this point, you should wait till the winter, dig them up, and divide each crown with a spade into 2-4 crowns. Replant the new crowns into separate pots, and leave for a year before harvesting again.

Blueberries

Blueberries will often do better in pots than they would in the ground. They're ericaceous (lime-hating) plants which require an acidic soil or ericaceous compost (available at any garden centre). This is much easier to handle in a pot than in open soil. Their shallow root systems also make them a good plant for container growing,

You get blueberry plants as young bushes. Put into a reasonably large pot (50-60cm, though it can survive in a 30cm pot but probably won't do so well) in ericaceous compost, and water regularly. Blueberries need plenty of water but hate having wet feet, so make sure the container drains well. An old ceramic sink can be a good option, as blueberries tend to have spreading rather than deep roots. Do NOT feed blueberries with any nitrate-containing fertiliser; you'll need to get hold of something specific for high-acid plants, or you may kill your plant. It should crop in midsummer, around July, although the exact time depends on your variety. Your first year's crop is likely (as with all fruit plants) to be small, but it should pick up thereafter. If you have birds around, net the plant or you'll lose the crop.

Over the winter, check the pH of the soil (pH is a measure of how acid or alkaline something is; lower values are more acidic, and 7 is neutral) with a soil testing kit, and add more of the acidic compost if the pH is above about 4.5 or 5 in order to lower the pH. You can also water with 1-2 tablespoons of vinegar in a gallon of water to change the pH.

Once it's well-established, you should also prune it during the autumn or winter. Aim to remove any overlapping branches/canes, and after the third year, you can start to remove the oldest branches, and any that look spindly or weak. You should remove about 15% of the old growth each year, to make way for new growth.

Citrus trees

Finally, you can even grow citrus trees in pots. Citrus generally are self-fertile, which means that you'll get fruit from even a single plant; so they're suitable for growing in small spaces. (Do confirm with the nursery that your specific species and variety is self-fertile before buying.)

Be warned, however, firstly that they're largely not very cold-hardy (if you're growing outside, pick a variety that is one of the more cold-hardy ones), and secondly, that in any given year you may or may not actually get a crop. My satsuma tree has flowered for two years in a row but so far none of the baby fruit have survived to maturity. I am hoping for better in future years! If you live somewhere moderately warm, and/or your space is south-facing; and you have a warm microclimate available, and you're able to cosset it a bit over the winter then it might be worth the effort. Alternatively, like me, you may simply be sufficiently keen on the idea that you feel that it's worth a go anyway.

Citrus trees can be bought online. You order them around this time of year to be delivered in mid-to-late spring, which is when they need to be planted out. Once established in their new home, water carefully but not too much – most citrus trees prefer to get a lot of water once in a while, rather than little and often. They may also require feeding. Check whatever information your tree came with for its specific requirements (lemon trees, for example, require frequent nitrogen-rich feeds between March and October). Make sure you site it in the warmest possible place, then keep your fingers crossed for some fruit.

The very beginnings of a satsuma fruit; unfortunately it didn't last (maybe next year...).

Remember that even a hardy citrus tree will need to be protected over winter (see p.44 for more on over-wintering delicate plants). A further protection for citrus trees is to avoid watering them between about December and March, as the worst thing for plants isn't so much cold as it is cold plus wet. The tree will survive the drought and recover in spring when you water it again and the weather warms up. You may also wish to fertilise it in the spring. You should expect it to take several years (or longer...) before you get a crop.

Rosemary

Rosemary is useful in the kitchen, medicinally useful, and impressively hardy, making it a great herb to grow in even a small space.

Growing

The easiest way to grow rosemary is from a cutting. Seeds are possible, but germination rates are low and the seeds don't always breed true to the parent. Find a friend who has a bush; or look out for a healthy-seeming rosemary bush in a nearby garden. Ask for a cutting, or if the plant is really enormous and jutting out into the street, it's arguably legitimate just to break off a couple of sprigs. Ideally, you should start off cuttings in late spring or early autumn, but it's worth a go at most times of the year.

Start off a couple of cuttings off rather than just one, in case one of them doesn't take. If you're happy to use rooting powder, that will improve its chances, but you can just stick each sprig into a small pot of compost each. They may well root happily anyway. Or see p.52 for how to make your own rooting compound from willow bark. Keep the pot on a sunny windowsill, and/or cut the top off a plastic bottle and put that over the cutting to act as a little propagator. Once your cutting is well-established and has started showing new growth, you should remove the plastic top and move the rosemary into a larger pot. Broadly speaking, the larger the pot, the larger your bush will eventually be, but you can of course transplant it again as it grows.

If you can't get hold of a cutting (or if you're impatient to get going!), you can buy a young plant from your local garden centre. Rosemary is hardy and very long-lived, so it's a one-off expense.

Rosemary, once established, grows well in most conditions. It prefers plenty of sun, but will tolerate some shade, and it likes well-drained soil. It's fairly hardy and frost resistant – it will survive winter happily in almost all

UK locations. Water whenever the soil is nearly dry, and harvest as you need it. Take from the tops of the twigs to encourage a more bushy habit (this may be useful in height-limited areas).

Culinary uses

Rosemary is great with roasted veg, or roasted potatoes in particular. Simply throw a couple of sprigs in with the veg to get a subtle flavour. Sage (see p.41) can also be nice in roasted veg. Rosemary is good chopped more finely in soups and stews, and is particularly nice with squash dishes and tomato dishes. You can even experiment with using a very small amount of rosemary in cakes or biscuits, and it's very good baked into bread.

Medicinal uses

Rosemary can help to relax digestive and uterus muscles, so using rosemary in cooking or drinking rosemary tea can help with digestive upset and menstrual cramps. It's also reputed to have a calming effect, and the tea can be used as a mild antiseptic. Rosemary essential oils are good for a hangover or for a headache, so the tea might be worth trying for a headache, too. Steep 1-2 teaspoons of crushed fresh herb in boiling water for 10 minutes to make the tea. The scent of rosemary is believed to be a memory stimulant, so keep a branch around when you're working!

Some recent studies suggest that rosemary contains some compounds which may help protect against free radicals in the brain, potentially lowering the risk of degenerative diseases such as Alzheimer's. Another study in rats demonstrated some potential anti-carcinogenic properties. However, these studies are at a very early stage.

Note that rosemary essential oil (as with most essential oils) should not be used directly on the skin, and if you use it in a bath be sure to stir it well in so it doesn't sit as a film on the water, or it may irritate your skin. Rosemary essential oil should on no account be taken internally. (Rosemary tea is fine.)

Pregnant and breastfeeding women should avoid consuming large quantities of rosemary, although it's fine used as a seasoning or in cooking.

CHAPTER 4

FEBRUARY

By February, you can finally start sowing seeds again, albeit only indoors. It's also a good time to make yourself some self-watering containers, ready for a couple of months' time.

· ·

My Balcony at the Start of February

Plants still alive and growing:

> **Herbs**: rosemary, thyme; bay, oregano, chives, and parsley (both flat and curly) in the cold frame. Basil plant inside.
>
> **Salad vegetables** on the railing: sorrel, bronze arrowhead lettuce, rocket.
>
> **Salad vegetables** in the other cold frame: bronze arrowhead lettuce, rocket.
>
> **Pak choi** perking up a bit.
>
> Several pots of small **broad bean** and **pea** plants.
>
> Two **mint** plants doing well.

Seeds and cuttings: none.

· ·

Things to Do in February

- Start broad beans and early peas (p.70).

- Start first sowings of lettuce and rocket inside (p.71).

- Make self-watering containers (p.73).

Sowing Time and Succession Sowing

As I'll discuss below, there are some early vegetables that you can start sowing now to add to anything you've overwintered. However, if you sow all your early vegetables now, then they'll grow early, crop early, and finish cropping early too – leaving you with nothing later.

To avoid this, you can succession sow. This means that instead of sowing all the seeds you want of a particular vegetable at the same time, you spread the sowing out over a period of a few weeks (or even a couple of months, depending on sowing season of the plant), and therefore spread the cropping season out over that time as well.

So you might sow a couple of early peas every week throughout February and March. Peas take between 12 and 15 weeks from sowing to harvesting, so your first lot, sowed in early February, will start producing peas in early June. The ones you sow at the start of April will start producing peas nearly two months later, at the start of August. Plants will keep producing peas for two to three weeks if you keep picking, which means that you'll get your first peas at the start of June and your last peas at the end of August – whereas if you were to sow all your seeds in late February, you'd get a glut of peas for the last couple of weeks of June and nothing outside that.

In fact, it's usually a bit more complicated than this. Seeds sown very early will take a bit longer to mature (although they will still start cropping early as well); seeds sown late may suffer in an unusually hot late spring and stop cropping a bit sooner (this has happened to my peas for a couple of years in a row). Different types of peas also naturally crop at different times (you can get early, mid, and late varieties). But you'll still extend the season at least a little. The other thing to bear in mind is that (if you're growing a small number of plants) your daily crop will be smaller with succession sowing, because it is spread out. What you prefer depends on whether you want, say, peas to nibble over a long time, or peas for dinner for four once or twice.

Even for cut-and-come-again plants such as (some types of) lettuce and rocket, succession sowing can be a good idea. You'll get early leaves alongside the more mature leaves, and the early plants will last a little longer before bolting. You can also do two sets of sowing: rocket does well in spring, and in late summer, but bolts immediately in mid-summer. So you can take a break from sowing it in late May / early June, then start again in early August.

Not all plants are suitable for succession sowing. Tomatoes, courgettes, and peppers for example, need quite a long time to produce fruit, so need to be sown as early as possible to give them a long growing season. (Tomatoes will also keep fruiting, if you're lucky, into October.) However, it may still be worth making a couple of sowings, separated by a week, in case something unfortunate happens to your first batch of seeds (a late frost, a marauding cat or dog...).

Early Vegetables

There are a few plants that can be started off as early as February:

- Broad beans do very well started early – you can even start them in November and leave them to overwinter. Plants will grow a little, then start off in earnest as the weather improves. See p.32 for more.

- Early peas also do very well started early (hence the name) – but you do need to grow specifically early varieties. Again, like broad beans, they'll be very slow until the conditions change, but then they're ready to shoot up the moment the weather improves. Snow peas can be sown in the autumn or in very early spring.

- Lettuce and rocket can be started now as well, for a very early crop. Succession sow from now onwards.

My collection of seedpots on the windowsill. Old fruit juice cartons are useful to protect the windowsill from water dripping.

Plants can be started off either outside, in the pot you wish them to end up in, or inside, in a smaller pot on a sunny windowsill. Hardy early vegetables such as broad beans and early peas needn't be started inside; but you may find that they germinate a bit faster that way. Sowing inside and hardening off is discussed below.

Frost dates

If you're starting to sow in February, you need to think carefully about frost dates. There's more about frost dates on p.28. Make sure that you don't move a plant outside that isn't ready for it.

Broad beans, as discussed above, can be started off outside and will survive frost. If starting them off inside, make sure to harden them off first by leaving them outside for a few hours in the middle of the day for a couple of days (then taking them in overnight) before moving them outside permanently. Failing to do this will stunt the plants' growth as they recover from the sudden shock of the change.

If in doubt, keep plants inside on your windowsill until you're certain that they're tough enough to survive or that the danger of frost is past. Even then, keep an eye on the forecast, as sudden late frosts are by no means unheard of even in southern England. If you're further north, this is even more important.

Starting seeds

In most cases (carrots and other root crops are the main exception), it's a good idea to start seeds off in a small pot, then transfer them to a larger one once they've got their first couple of sets of true leaves. This makes them more transportable, and means that you can start them off inside on a protected windowsill, in your sunniest/most protected position outside, or in a portable greenhouse. You can fit a much higher number of baby plants in small pots into the space available for starting seeds off than if you sow directly into the larger pots you'll use later.

You may be able to get small seed pots from gardener friends (they seem to proliferate at a great rate at my allotment, and there are always piles on the give-away table). Alternatively, you can make your own out of paper or newspaper. Rip the paper into strips slightly taller than you want the seed pots to be, wrap each strip around a suitably sized round thing (a 500ml water bottle, or a rolling pin if you want very small pots), and tape it to hold it closed. Remove the cylinder from whatever you wrapped it around, and fold over and tape one end to construct a bottom. Fill with compost, and insert your plant.

These seed pots won't survive for all that long, but they should last for long enough to get the plants started. In theory, when you transplant the plant you can put the whole thing, paper and all, straight into the compost, and the paper will decompose as the plant grows. However, in my experience, plants do much less well this way than if you carefully remove the paper, as their roots struggle to escape. It may be that it depends how tough your paper is, so actual newsprint might be more successful; or it may be that the paper decomposes more slowly in pots without the insect assistance that you'd get in soil. I have found that it's much better to gently remove the paper before carefully putting the baby plant into its new home.

Self-Watering Containers

As discussed in the Introduction (p.24), one of the big problems for container gardeners is making sure that their plants are watered often enough and well enough, as otherwise your plants just won't do as well as they might. One way of helping ensure that thirsty plants such as tomatoes never run out of water is to make self-watering containers.

The basic idea is that you have a main container, which has earth and the plant in, and then underneath that there is a reservoir of water. A wick between the two (a piece of string or cloth, or ideally a small holey container, a bit like a colander, filled with earth and hung into the reservoir) brings the water up to the plant. Refill the reservoir regularly, and the plant will never go thirsty. I'm told that SWCs can massively increase plant yield, although with my own small space it's hard to test that properly. My tomatoes in SWCs did seem to do a little better than the others, though, and my best-producing plant was in an SWC as well as against a south-facing wall.

Two-litre or three-litre plastic bottles can make single-plant SWCs for small plants. Alternatively, you can use larger containers – I've made several SWCs from 30cm plant tubs, as described overleaf.

When you water the pot, water it very thoroughly. The excess water will drain through the plant pot at the bottom, into the bottom tub, creating a pool of water. As the earth further up dries out, water will be wicked up via the earth in the plant pot, as the plant needs it.

73

Plastic Bottle Self-watering Container

Materials: 2 litre plastic bottle.

Piece of an old cotton T-shirt, around 20 x 20cm.

Compost.

Sharp knife.

Sandpaper (for sharp edges).

Marker pen (to mark fill line).

Steps:

A row of bottle SWCs. The tomat
were a bit too restricted in these
but the chard did well.

1. Cut the plastic bottle in half 13cm from the bottom. It doesn't matter if the line is a bit wavy. The top half (with the neck) will be the planting container; the bottom half will be the water reservoir.

2. Sand down the cut edges, then wash off the bottles to remove any plastic dust.

3. You can if you want paint the top half of the bottle (which will be the planting container). Some people reckon that this helps protect the roots. (I have never bothered, as I have never had paint lying around.)

4. Take the cotton wick, and push it through the neck of the bottle so half is inside the bottle and the other half is outside. Wet it all down (to help it start wicking).

5. Put the planting container, neck-down, into the water reservoir. They should fit neatly together.

6. Add the compost, a little at a time, to the bottom of the planting container. Pull the wick up as you put the compost in, so it's surrounded by the compost, and damp the compost down as you put it in.

7. Put in your plant at the appropriate time (or fill it all the way up then add the seeds), just like you normally would when repotting or sowing seeds, (see p.82).

8. Water the plant in and tamp down the compost.

9. Look at where the neck of the bottle is in relation to the water reservoir. You should be filling to about halfway up the neck, so that the wick is all that's in contact with the water. Mark this on the outside of the reservoir with the marker pen.

10. Take the planting container out, fill up the reservoir to the mark with water, and put the container back in again. You can also water by watering from the top and letting the water drain through.

11. Make sure you check the water reservoir regularly and refill when needed!

Florists' Tub Self-watering Container

A basic and cheap style of self-watering container, suitable for one tomato plant, can be made using florists' tubes, as follows.

Materials: Two florists' tubs (my local florist will sell them off at 10 for £1).
They should be the sort without drainage holes in the bottom.
A small plastic plant pot (5-10cm across, and significantly smaller than the width of the base of the florists' tubs).
Sharp knife.
Empty plastic bottles (or anything else that will suit the job they're doing – see below).

Steps:

1. Cut a round hole in the centre of the base of one of the florists' tubs. The plant pot should sit just inside the hole (sticking out through the bottom of the florist's tub, but not falling through), so the diameter of the hole needs to be just smaller than the diameter of the top of the plant pot (see photo).

Bottom half of the SWC, with the plastic bottles to hold the top half up.

2. Punch or drill a few holes around the base and sides of the small plant pot, to allow water to soak through. Drilling may work better, as the holes should be a couple of mm across.

3. Cut the base off two water bottles. The height of the cut off bases should be slightly greater than the height of the small plant pot.

4. Take your second florist's tub (the one that doesn't have a big hole in the bottom), and place the water bottles inside its base. These will provide something for the first tub to rest on, so that when you stack the two tubs together, there's a space between their bases for the water to live in. Stack the first tub in on top, so it rests on the water bottles.

Top half of the SWC, with the hole-filling plant pot sitting at the bottom.

5. Push the plant pot into place inside the hole cut for it in the first tub. You now have two florist's tubs stacked together, with a space between them to act as a water reservoir, and a plant pot which drops down into that space and which will soak up the water from the reservoir as needed, through the holes you drilled in it.

6. Depending on the design of the florists' tubs, you may need to put a little packing material around the edge where the tubs are stacked in each other, to prevent the top tub from wobbling. Cardboard will do for this (although may disintegrate over time); or a rolled up piece of scrap plastic. On one occasion I found that the top of the cut up water bottle fitted very neatly; basically, see what you can fish out of your rubbish bin! See the photo below.

The two halves put together, with a cork to wedge them so they don't shift around.

7. Carefully pack compost down into the plant pot, before filling the rest of the tub (leave filling the whole tub until you actually have a plant to put in it).

It's important that the base of the plant pot should be very nearly sitting at the bottom of the bottom tub, so it can wick up all the water sitting there. Another option when watering is to fit a spout that will directly feed the reservoir, but I've never found that to be necessary.

My experience is that water-hungry plants like tomatoes do incredibly well in these – it means that you can get away with only watering every couple of days, rather than every day, even in very hot weather. Every time a tomato plant loses enough water to droop, you're affecting its growth and the growth of the fruit. Using self-watering containers means that (if you keep watering regularly) the plant will never run out of water, and you'll get higher yields and tastier fruit.

There are far more complicated versions of self-watering containers available to buy, or you can look online for more complicated patterns involving Rubbermaid plastic tubs. The important parts, though, are a space to act as a reservoir, and some way of wicking up the water from that reservoir. Experiment with your own structures on this basis!

HERB OF THE MONTH

Parsley

There are two main sorts of parsley: curly and flat. The curly stuff is prettier, but the taste of the flat parsley is better, so if you want to use it for cooking rather than for decoration, grow flat leaved parsley.

Growing

Parsley isn't too difficult to grow from seed, but it does have a very long germination period (3-4 weeks), and requires warm temperatures. You're likely to have more success starting it off inside somewhere warm than sowing it directly outside, especially if starting in spring. On several occasions I've sown parsley outside in spring and haven't seen anything of it until midsummer, when the temperature finally rose high enough for it to germinate. Since the germination is a bit tricky, sow several seeds per seed pot, and remove all but the strongest seedling by snipping them off at soil level with a pair of scissors.

Once the seedlings are well-established, harden them off for a couple of days, then transplant them into their new pots. Parsley can do well in reasonably small pots, and it likes a well-drained, damp soil. It also requires nutrient-rich compost to get good-tasting leaves, so, unlike a lot of herbs, will require a certain amount of feeding. It prefers a decent amount of light (around 6 hours/day) but will tolerate partial shade.

One of the nice things about parsley is that it self-seeds like mad. So once you've got your first parsley plant established, it will take care of things for you after that. (This can get a bit out of hand; but you can always eat any parsley seedlings that you have to pull up!) It's biennial, so it won't set seed until its second full year. You'll get a full year's growth out of your first plant, before it flowers and sets seed at some point in the second year.

Culinary uses

Parsley is an incredibly versatile cooking herb. Its fresh flavour makes it a good addition to all sorts of meals. It's a standard addition to a *bouquet garni* mix, and is used in *fines herbs* (a French mixture used in various dishes, which also includes chervil, chives, and tarragon). It's used a lot in Middle Eastern cooking, and is great with chickpeas and in salads. Broadly speaking: if in doubt, add a little parsley to what you're cooking! It is also a nice garnish, but it's a waste just to use it for this when you could eat it as well. It goes particularly well with lemon. Chewing parsley is also said to freshen your breath after eating garlic!

Medicinal uses

Parsley has high levels of iron, carotene, and various other vitamins, so is therefore a good thing to eat in its own right. Parsley root is more often used than the leaves in herbal medicine, as a treatment for rheumatism and also to promote menstruation and relieve menstrual pain. The leaves can also be used for this, but this may be a bit less effective.

Parsley tea may help relieve bladder infections and cystitis; and can help digestion. But parsley can be a little irritating to the kidneys, and so should be avoided by those with kidney problems and pregnant women (as a medicine; it's fine to eat in small quantities as a culinary herb).

CHAPTER 5

MARCH

By March, things are starting to kick off again in earnest. There are lots of seeds to start, early seedlings to harden out and plant off, and potatoes to chit. This is the first of the busiest few gardening months!

· ·

My Balcony at the Start of March

Plants and seedlings:

Herbs:

Rosemary, **thyme**, **bay**, **oregano**, and **parsley** (both flat and curly), all still in the large cold frame, but nearly time to move them all out again.

Chives just starting to grow back (chives die down over winter).

Basil still hanging in there on the windowsill, looking a little sorry for itself.

Mint cuttings doing well.

Salad vegetables on the railing and in the small cold frame:

Bronze arrowhead lettuce.

Rocket.

Sorrel unfortunately died in February.

Pak choi: a couple of plants looking a little sad.

Bean and **pea** seedlings.

Seeds and cuttings:

Rocket and **lettuce** seedlings showing.

Br ar let seed

Miscellaneous Other:

Black plastic sack of leaves, in the process of becoming **leafmould**: these were quite dry when I checked on them and needed a little dampening down.

Wormery: lots of compost, worms looking a little dry so I added some water – this shouldn't need to be done very often, since as long as the contents are slightly damp the worms will be OK.

Self-watering containers awaiting tomatoes and peppers.

Things to Do in March

- Pack away the cold frames (p.36).

- Regenerate your potting compost (p.80).

- Plant out any overwintered peas and beans (p.82).

- Further succession sowing of lettuce and rocket (p.84).

- Sow carrots (p.88).

- Sow first sowings of spinach beet and chard (p.92).

- Sow chillies, peppers, and aubergines on a windowsill (p.94).

- Chit potatoes (p.97).

- Sow tomatoes on the windowsill if you're in the south (p.106).

- Herbs: sow sage indoors (p.41), oregano indoors (p.101), chives indoors or outdoors (p.123), basil indoors (p.143), ginger indoors (p.180).

- Chive division (p.123).

Potting Compost

The potting compost you tidied up in November (see p.176) has now been sitting around in its plastic bag all winter, and probably drying out a bit. It's time now to revitalise it so you can use it for this year's crops. Although compost manufacturers will tell you to buy new compost every year, in fact experiments carried out by gardening magazines found that you can use compost at least two years in a row (though you may need to add more liquid feed the second year). Mix it through with some new compost and you can keep it going for longer. However, you may need to get its water content back up a bit before putting plants into it, if it's dried out over the winter.

Some people (myself included) are happy to keep reusing their compost indefinitely, mixing each year with a healthy quantity of fresh compost, either from a shop or from your compost heap or compost worms. Others prefer to use it for at most two or three years and then switch it in for new. Your preference may in part depend on whether you can readily dispose of old compost (e.g. if you have access to an allotment or someone with a garden).

If you have any diseases in your plants, you must get rid of the compost in those pots or risk transferring the disease to the next year's plants. It is also a good idea to mix the compost around a bit (i.e. don't just keep planting tomatoes in the same pot of the same compost year after year) to reduce the chances of incubating a plant-specific disease.

If you're lucky, your worms have been working busily away all winter, and you can pull out a quantity of nice fresh worm compost. See p.33 for information on setting up a wormery. Once you've got it out, open up the bag of last year's compost, and mix in the new worm compost a trowelful at a time. While you're doing this, if the compost feels dry and dusty, tip in a little water with each trowelful of worm compost. You're aiming to get the compost back to roughly how it felt when it was new (damp and tending to stick to itself), as well as boosting its nutrient level. Once you've mixed it all through, add a little more water, and leave it to sit for a day or two. If it's dried out a lot, you may have to add more water again after a couple of days. Dry compost won't hold the water that your new plants will need.

If you don't have worm compost, you can do the same thing by adding a little new potting compost to the old. Throwing the whole lot away and replacing it simply isn't necessary, and is very wasteful (not to mention expensive).

Do, however, remember that firstly, if you've grown anything with a tendency to self-seed (rocket is particularly notorious for this, as is parsley), you may find that you get volunteer seedlings in your pots. If you're bothered by this, buy a small bag of fresh sterile compost to start seedlings off in. Once they're well established, sharing their larger pot with the odd volunteer won't matter too much (and you can just snip the volunteers out).

Secondly, some of the goodness (fertility) of the old compost will have been used up last year. The worm compost will help with that, but you will also need to feed more than you might with fresh compost. You can buy organic plant food from a garden centre, or you can make your own from nettles or comfrey, see p.119 for more information.

If you're making a compost mix for pots from scratch, rather than just mixing in a little new compost with your old mix, see the discussion of potting mixes on p.21.

Getting an Early Start

By the start of March, anything you've overwintered in cold frames (or even out of them, in the case of some hardy lettuces) should be starting to perk up a bit. One of the major advantages of overwintering plants is that you get a head start on their production for the next year, even if you can't crop all that much over the winter itself.

In the south of the UK, the last frost date isn't until late April. This means that you need to be careful with sowing or moving delicate plants outside until late April. Tomatoes, peppers, and other similar plants may all be killed by a late frost. However, there are plenty of plants that are sufficiently hardy to cope with the sort of mild frosts that are all you're likely to get by late March. Additionally, depending on the layout of your space, you may find that you have a microclimate that is a little warmer than the general temperature – for example, a protected or south-facing balcony. Being above ground can reduce the chance of frost, as the air tends to be a little warmer than the ground, but certain weather conditions can produce an 'air frost', so you shouldn't rely on this.

By mid-March in southern areas you can start to dismantle your cold frames, to get the plants used to life in the outside world. If you're a long way north, you may want to leave this until a little later. Basically, you should be able to get your plants out of the cold frames a month or so before your last frost date, or a couple of weeks after you notice them starting to perk up more than they were over winter.

Peas and Beans

Planting out seedlings

If you sowed peas or beans in November (see p.32) into small pots, it's definitely time now to plant them out into larger pots – indeed, you may even want to think about doing this at the end of February, in areas further south. You can put three or four pea or bean plants in a 35cm pot, if you're careful to feed and water them regularly. See p.87 for more discussion of plant spacing.

Overwintered peas and beans ready to be moved into larger pots.

Before you take each pea seedling out of its pot, first prepare its larger pot. Put compost in until the surface of the compost is roughly the height of the small pot below the top of the larger pot. So if your seedling is in a 10cm tall pot, fill in your larger pot to about 11cm below the top of the pot. Compost tends to settle, so in the end you'll want to fill the larger pot fairly close to its top.

To get the seedling out of its pot without damaging it, spread your fingers around the base of the plant, just above the earth, and cup your hand over the surface of the pot. Turn the whole thing upside-down, and gently pull the pot off. If the roots are showing around the edges of the earth, very gently tease them out just a little, without breaking them, to encourage them to grow outwards when they're in the new pot. Put the whole thing on top of the compost in the middle of the larger pot and then start filling in around it with more compost. When it's all the way to the top, water it in well, and make sure you add a label! Ideally, labelling it with the date of planting out is good, but at the least, it's best to give it an identity, especially if you have lots of different varieties of a particular plant. Later on, you may want to know which brand of pea was the best-producing, for example.

If you have several seedlings in one pot, you can very gently move the earth away from around them and tease them apart from each other. Do your best to do as little damage to the roots as possible – this is one good reason for using single small pots for seedlings you intend to plant on. In this case, you'll probably want to fill the larger pot all the way up to the top, and then make a hole in it for each plant. Make sure the hole is much bigger (in both width and depth) than the root system of the plant you're putting into it, and then fill in around the plant to keep it upright.

If your seedlings have been living inside, you'll need to harden them off before you put them out full-time. You do this by putting them out for a few hours each day for a few days, then taking them back inside, before leaving them out overnight for the first time. If you just put them straight outside, the shock of the temperature change (particularly overnight) will slow their growth, and may even mean that you lose the benefit of having planted them early.

Harvesting

Towards the end of April, your peas should start getting big enough to harvest. One of the very nice things about peas and beans is that the more you harvest from them, the more they'll grow – if, on the other hand, you let the pods stay on the plants, they'll stop producing more.

This is generally true for most fruiting plants and cut-and-come-again plants: the more you harvest, the more they'll grow. Peas, of course, despite counting as 'vegetables', are in fact a seed, so they have more in common with fruiting plants than they do with root vegetables.

Freshly harvested peas with a baby carrot.

You may find that very early peas can be eaten pod and all; but they won't be so nice for this as mangetout (you'll want to plant out your mangetout seedlings this month but won't be harvesting until next month). It's better to wait a week or so until the pods plump up a bit, indicating that the peas inside have grown to a decent size. Fresh peas can be steamed or boiled very briefly; or you can just eat them neat. The pods, of course, go straight back into the compost.

Lettuce and Other Green Leaves

Even if you overwintered some of your lettuce, and certainly if you didn't, you'll probably want to start sowing some fresh seeds now, so you can keep on getting fresh leaves as the overwintered plants (especially the rocket) go to seed in a few weeks.

Types of lettuce

For the purposes of the home gardener, there are two important distinctions between different lettuce types: loose leaf (cut-and-come-again) lettuce, and hearted lettuce. With hearted lettuce, the plant grows and matures all at once, so you pick the whole thing and eat it at one time. Cos, romaine, crisphead (such as Iceberg) and butterhead are all hearted lettuces. Loose leaf lettuce, on the other hand, does not form a heart, but instead just grows a succession of loose leaves. You can take a few leaves from the plant at a time and it will keep growing; hence 'cut and come again'. There are a huge number of varieties of loose leaf; lollo rosso is particularly well known, but one of my favourites for home growing is bronze arrowhead lettuce. Royal oak leaf also has good writeups for taste.

For growing in pots, loose leaf lettuce, in one or several of its many varieties, is far and away the best choice. You can pick leaves over a longer period, and the plant will keep producing; with headed lettuces, it's an all or nothing deal. This also means that you can give them less space – the plants will stay small, but they'll keep producing leaves (just small ones), whereas a hearted variety would struggle to succeed at all. However, if you're particularly fond of headed lettuce, by all means give it a go!

Bronze arrowhead lettuce seedlings.

Lettuce of all sorts is at its best in cooler weather, so get it started as early in the season as you can to maximise the yield before the weather gets too hot and it starts to bolt.

Baby greens going to seed.

Lettuces aren't the only green leaf salad veg plant available, either. One of the best things to grow in a small space is rocket. It costs a fortune in the shops, comes washed in chlorine with half its flavour gone, and grows as a weed in this country, so it's pretty easy to grow! It was brought over by the Romans around 2,000 years ago and has been thriving here ever since. You can buy either wild or domestic rocket seeds (domestic has a slightly milder flavour), and you can treat them much like lettuce when sowing. See p.140 for a discussion of the problem of bolting; in general, the best bet is to sow early in the season for a pre-midsummer crop, and then in about July for the rest of the summer (and on into winter if you have a cold frame, see p.36).

You could also try sorrel, which is, as a rule, perennial (although mine died over a particularly cold winter). Its lemony leaves have a lovely light flavour, and it's another prolific cropper, given half a chance. A couple of sorrel plants are likely to be plenty.

Young chard leaves can be nice in salad (see p.92 for a discussion of growing chard). You can also try land cress, or some of the more exotic green leaves such as mizuna. Check the seed packet for specific growing instructions, but in general all of these green leafy plants can be treated in much the same way as described for lettuces.

Sowing green leaves

Lettuces and green leaves of all sorts are sown in much the same way: sow the seed fairly thinly (see below about thinning later on) and cover very lightly. A good rule of thumb is that the seed should be sown at about its own depth; so tiny rocket or lettuce seeds barely need to be covered at all. Water in and keep moist. Most green leaves are fairly quick to germinate, so you should see signs of life in a week or so (a bit longer if it's cold). They are happy to germinate outside or inside – I always sow mine outside to save any transplantation hassle. If you

Self-seeded rocket seedlings.

don't have any overwintered leaves, you may prefer to start inside to get going a little earlier. In this case, be careful to harden them off gradually when you move them outside.

Spacing and thinning

You have two choices when you're sowing lettuce (or indeed any other plant): sow straight to the desired spacing, or sow more thickly and then thin out later on once they've come up. Sowing straight to the desired spacing has the advantage that you avoid both more work later on, and wasting seeds; but if you're sowing something like lettuce that is edible as soon as it starts to grow, thinning isn't so much 'work' as it is 'harvesting', and indeed 'food'.

Given that, I usually sow lettuce more thickly than I'll want them when they reach their final size, and aim to thin them out and eat the thinnings as they grow. You should always use a pair of scissors to thin out plants, by cutting them off just above the ground; if you just pull them out, you may uproot or damage the roots of other plants that you wanted to keep, especially if they're particularly thickly sown.

When thinning, decide the spacing you want to have when you've finished, and then choose the strongest plant and thin those around it until you reach the desired spacing. With lettuce, and other plants with edible thinnings, you can thin more than once to maximise the food yield. Take out some extraneous seedlings at a very early stage, and leave the rest of the plants to grow a little more. Then thin again when they start to look crowded, and eat this more robust second set of thinnings. If you thin all at once early on, you won't get this extra harvest. Very young lettuce and other green leaf plants are known as 'microgreens' and are quite trendy right now (as well as very tasty!). Microgreens can in fact be grown all year round on a windowsill – see p.128 for more on this – and can also be used as a catch crop. Scatter a few seeds in the pot where, for example, you intend to put your tomatoes later on, and you'll have time for a crop of microgreens before it's time to move the tomatoes in. You may even be able to leave some of the lettuce plants in around the foot of the tomato, when you do plant it out.

It's also worth bearing in mind that the spacing given on the packet may be quite generous anyway, especially since if you're growing cut-and-come-again lettuce, they don't need the space to form a big 'heart' that hearted varieties do. Thicker plant coverage also means less bare ground and thus less room for weeds (even balconies can end up with weeds from air- or bird-borne seeds). You can also always thin further later on if the plants begin to look overcrowded (and again, eat the thinnings). I tend to sow loose leaf lettuce within 7.5-10cm of one another even when they're fully grown, and take more plants out only if they seem overcrowded (or just eat the leaves faster). In a shallow pot, where their growth will be restricted due to the restrictions on their roots, you can reduce that a little further. Do remember though that they'll need plenty of food and water.

Carrots

Growing in pots isn't particularly good for large carrots – it's possible, but you need deep pots and won't get many carrots per pot. It's great, however, if you're after baby carrots, and you can also get some dwarf or stumpy varieties that can get reasonably big in pots. It's best to think, before making a decision, about your carrot preferences and the best use of your space. You'll get a higher number of baby carrots per pot, and as you pull them up, you can start sowing new ones, so over the season you can get a consistent supply. Main crop carrots need longer to grow, so this approach won't work so well for them – you can expect only a single crop per pot. Baby or dwarf carrots are also more expensive to buy in the shops, and the freshness of home-grown just-pulled carrots is more likely to show up in these varieties. Having said all that, if you don't eat raw baby carrots then there's no point in growing them!

Sowing and germinating

I confess that I've always had trouble with carrots, both in the allotment and on the balcony, although the year I was writing this book I finally managed a carrot harvest in both locations. Carrot gemination seems to be surprisingly challenging for such a staple crop. Part of the problem is that they are slow to germinate – up to three weeks before the shoots will emerge from the ground. So do be patient! This can make them more vulnerable to slugs and snails, as well. One advantage of growing in pots is that it's easier to keep them away from these pests (try a hanging container, or use copper tape around the edge of the pot, if necessary);

and on a balcony or roof, slugs are usually just not a problem at all. Carrot germination can also be spotty, as well as slow. In my experience it's well worth sowing more thickly than you want, to allow for this erratic germination rate, especially since carrot seed only lasts a single season anyway (so you may as well use the whole packet). Finally, in order to germinate, carrot seeds must be kept moist, so make sure you keep an eye on them and water regularly so that the soil doesn't dry out.

Carrot seedlings just coming up.

Another tip is to freeze the seeds before sowing them (so they experience a greater 'warmth' when sown, which encourages germination). In my not entirely scientific experiments this year, this didn't seem to make a difference in the germination rate, but it's an easy thing to try so may be worth a go.

Carrots, like most root vegetables, don't like to be disturbed once they've started growing, as this will break all the tiny rootlets that emerge from the surface of the main root (the carrot itself). So you need to sow them *in situ*, or to start them in seed plugs and move them as a whole block (earth and all) when you plant them out. If you like, you can experiment with both.

As carrot seeds are so tiny, they barely need to be covered after sowing. Just sprinkle a very little compost over them and water in well. If sowing directly into a pot, sow fairly thickly and be prepared to thin them once they come up. As mentioned above, the seeds must be kept moist while they're germinating. One way I've seen suggested to make this a little easier to manage is to moisten the soil after you sow them, and then cover it with something to keep the moisture in (plastic, old carpet, old T-shirts, skip-rescue plywood...anything that will prevent the soil from drying out). Keep checking for germination, and remove the covering once the plants are starting to show. I did try this, but didn't see any difference in germination success compared to my uncovered pots.

Once the seedlings are an inch or two high, thin to an inch or so apart, keeping the strongest seedlings and using a pair of scissors to cut out the weaker ones (don't just pull them out, as this risks disturbing the remaining seedlings, and the thinnings won't be worth eating at this stage). Later, you can gradually thin them out further, before they start crowding one another but after the thinnings are worth nibbling at, by pulling every other carrot.

Harvesting

If you want to keep your carrot provision going for a bit longer, you can try sowing more seed in the gaps left as you harvest a handful of carrots at a time. Carrots can be sown for most of the spring and early summer, although won't do so well over the hottest part of the summer. Indeed, some people recommend sowing in early summer to maximise germination rates. In theory, you can also sow again in late summer for an early autumn crop, if you have any seed left, but I haven't myself had great success with this.

Carrot fly

If you're growing on a balcony, you shouldn't have problems with this notorious pest, since carrot fly don't get more than 60cm above the ground. If you're growing on a patio, you may want to consider using a plank of wood and a couple of bricks (or tin cans) to put your carrot pots on, to raise the carrots above fly level. You can also net the carrots, but you need a very fine net to stop the flies. There are no organic pesticides available for carrot fly (although a nematode treatment is new on the market), so you're far better off trying simply to avoid the problem. Sow thinly and in early summer to minimise problems if you do experience difficulty with carrot fly, or try interplanting with other veg to confuse the flies.

Beetroot

Beetroot is another root that can be readily grown in containers, although you may not get such large beets as you might in the ground. To maximise your crop, you can also eat the beet greens, but see below for members of the beet family that are grown specifically for greens. As with carrots (and any other root vegetables that you want to grow), you'll need a reasonably deep pot to grow worthwhile beets, although you can grow baby beets in troughs or shallower pots.

Sowing and thinning

Like carrots, beetroot are best sown directly into the pot which is their final destination. They germinate more reliably than carrots, though, so you can sow them more thinly. Sow them in mid-spring (they're not frost-hardy, so wait until after the final frost), to about the depth of half a fingernail (1-1.5cm) and around 5cm apart and cover over with soil, then water in. The bigger you want your beets to be when you harvest them, the deeper the pot you'll need. Very shallow pots aren't suitable at all.

Beetroot will normally take a couple of weeks to germinate. Beetroot seed come up in little clusters, so shortly after they first appear you'll need to snip out all but one plant from each cluster. Thin them again when they're about 7cm tall, to a spacing of 10-15cm apart.

You can keep succession sowing every couple of weeks until mid-summer (and possibly a little later in mild areas) to get an ongoing crop.

Keep them well-watered, and feed a little if your compost needs it. Don't over-water, or you'll get more greens and less root.

Harvesting and eating

Beets take 8-10 weeks to mature, and you should be able to see how big the roots are getting as they poke up above the ground a little. Pull from the base of the leaf cluster and they should come up easily. As mentioned above, you can also eat beet greens, treated much like spinach when cooking.

Seed saving

Beet is wind-pollinated and will cross with other beet-like plants, so you can only reliably save seed if you aren't growing any other types of chard or beet yourself, and there are no other similar plants within ¼ mile (this distance may be a little less in heavily built-up urban areas with few gardens around). In practice, this often makes seed saving impractical, but it may be worth a go if you're not growing anything else. Alternatively, you can try fastening a large paper bag over the flower heads to protect them from cross-pollination. To improve pollination if you're doing this, shake the bags up regularly to move the (very light) pollen around within the bag.

The seed will set the year after sowing, so keep the plants sheltered over the winter, and wait for the seed heads to grow in late spring or early summer the next season. In southern areas beet should survive the winter easily (the leaves are likely to die down over the coldest part of the winter, then return in the spring); in northern areas it may need a cold frame or other protection.

Be warned that the flower heads can grow to well over a metre! You'll probably need to stake them. Once the seeds have set, harvest the stalks as they dry and collect the large round seeds.

Spinach Beet and Chard

Spinach beet and chard are both members of the beetroot family that are grown for their leaves rather than for their roots. They're cut-and-come-again plants, so are very well-suited to growing in pots, because you maximise the return you get per plant. Chard in particular is also cold-hardy, so once you have the plant going, you may be able to keep it going right through the winter and into the next season.

The size of the leaves is dependent on the depth to which the root can sink, so if you sow chard or spinach beet in shallow troughs, the plants will grow, but you'll get only small leaves. If you pick these early, they can be nice in salads. If you want larger leaves, you'll need deeper pots.

Sowing and thinning

Like carrots and beet, chard and spinach beet are best sown directly into the pot which is their final destination. They germinate more reliably than carrots, though, so you can sow them more thinly. Sow them to about the depth of half a fingernail (1-1.5cm) and around 5cm apart and cover over with soil, then water in. If you use a deep pot, you'll get larger leaves, as the root has more room to grow; if you want small leaves, you can sow in a trough or shallower pot.

The time taken for the plants to start to come up varies according to temperature, from 6 weeks at 5°C to only a couple of weeks at around 15°C. However, chard are cold-hardy, so there's no need to worry about sowing too early – the worst that will happen is that you'll have to wait longer for them to germinate.

When the plants do start to come up, you may find that you get multiple plants apparently from the same seed, or at least very close together. If this happens, then when the baby plants start showing their first proper leaves, pick the strongest plant from each cluster, and carefully snip the others off using nail scissors. Don't just tug them out, or you'll disturb the root system of the plant you want to keep.

If you want small leaves, you may not need to thin them any further. However, if you thin every other plant when they reach 15cm or so in height, you can eat the thinnings, then leave the rest to use as cut-and-come-again plants. Chard is quite tolerant of overcrowding, so you should be able to get away with 10cm between plants even once they're quite large. Plants in a shallower pot, which will grow smaller leaves, can be significantly closer together than this.

You can keep succession sowing every few weeks until the early autumn, or just keep harvesting leaves as needed and the plant will keep producing more. Water regularly to avoid the leaves becoming bitter.

Harvesting and eating

Harvesting is easy: once the leaves are large enough (around 7.5cm), simply take hold of the leaf as low down the stalk as you can reach, and twist it off. Harvest from the outside, and more leaves will grow from the inside. Later on in the season, if outer leaves become damaged by frost, the inner leaves will be protected and can still be eaten, which is great during autumn and winter. Mark the best plants for later seed saving if you may want to do that.

One of the best ways to eat larger chard or spinach beet leaves is to flash fry them. Separate the leaves from the stalk, and chop them both crossways into strips about a centimetre thick. Dice a little garlic and ginger finely, and heat some oil. Throw in the garlic and ginger, then the chopped stalks. Add the leaves after about a minute, and after another minute, splash in a tablespoon of soy sauce, stir quickly, and serve.

Small leaves can be eaten as salad.

Seed saving

As with beet, chard is wind-pollinated and will cross with other chards and beets, so you can only reliably save seed if you aren't growing any other types of chard or beet yourself, and there are no other similar plants within ¼ mile (this distance may be a little less in heavily built-up urban areas with few gardens around). In practice, this often makes seed saving impractical, but if you aren't growing any other chard, spinach, or beet yourself and aren't near other gardens, it may be worth a go. Alternatively, you can try fastening a large paper bag over the flower heads to protect them from cross-pollination. To improve pollination if you're doing this, shake the bags up regularly to move the (very light) pollen around within the bag.

The seed will set the year after sowing, so keep the plants sheltered over the winter, and wait for the seed heads to grow in late spring or early summer the next season. In southern areas chard should survive the winter easily; in northern areas it may need a cold frame or other protection.

Once the seeds have set, harvest the stalks as they dry and collect the large round seeds.

I've never successfully seed-saved chard seeds that breed true (I haven't yet tried the paper bag technique), but I've had some interesting self-seeded chard/spinach crosses show up in my allotment from time to time! They tend to run to seed much faster than their parents and the quality of the leaves unfortunately varies widely.

Chillies, Peppers and Aubergines

It's possible to grow chillies, sweet peppers, and aubergines in pots in the UK, but unfortunately we don't really have the climate to make it easy. The problem is that these plants need a extended period of long and sunny days for their fruit to ripen, which they may not get in the UK. If you sow at all late, they certainly won't get this, and you won't get a crop.

To maximise your chances of success, sow as early as possible, on a sunny windowsill, and let the seedlings grow on inside for a while.

In the UK, you really need to sow an early variety, and by the middle of March at the latest, to have a chance of a decent crop. (Real Seeds sell some good early varieties, see p.192 for details.)

If you have any kind of cover available (such as a mini-greenhouse), chillies in particular will do much better there. However, Real Seeds do have a couple of 'outdoor' varieties which are a bit easier to ripen, and if you have a sunny, south-facing space then an early-ripening chilli may well fruit well anyway. Alternatively, you could just keep them on a sunny windowsill throughout the summer.

Chillies will do better under cover.

If you're going to grow the plants outside, don't move them out until the seedlings are a decent size, and definitely not until well past any danger of frost is past. It's also important to make sure that you harden them off. Put them outside for only a couple of hours in the middle of the day at first, then bring them back in. Gradually extend the time they stay out over the next few days, until you leave them outside overnight for the first time, after which they can stay outside.

The good news is that once your plants are established, in the right conditions, both sweet peppers and chilli peppers are in theory perennials. In cold UK conditions, they will usually die over the winter, but if you protect them or bring them inside then they ought to survive. I have once managed to overwinter a couple of sweet pepper plants outside, which meant that they started producing fruit much earlier in the season in the second year, and I got a fairly respectable crop of smallish peppers. Unfortunately the next winter was just a little too cold for them. See p.44 for ideas of how to protect delicate plants like these from the cold, or take them inside when it starts to get cold in October or November. If I were overwintering sweet peppers again, I would bring them indoors. Overwintering chilli peppers indoors is straightforward –

I've done this for a couple of years in a row.

I've only tried growing an aubergine once, and the single tiny fruit I got didn't encourage me to have another go. Other people have been more successful, and it is possible to get a few aubergines from a plant in the UK (if you're in the far north, this is likely to be harder, as they really do need warm conditions). Your success rate is likely to be related even more than usual to the weather conditions (a cold or a hot summer), so it's very hit and miss unless you have a mini-greenhouse, which will make a crop much more likely. If growing outside (even in a warm microclimate) expect one fruit from a large-fruited variety, and maybe three from a small-fruited variety. If you can grow them inside a mini-greenhouse you may be able to double this.

Sowing and planting out

Sowing any of these plants inside is exactly the same as for tomatoes. Sow either one seed to a compost plug, or a couple of seeds to a small pot, and then plant them up into bigger pots as required. You'll probably want to move the plants to 7.5cm pots in April, and then into 20 or 23cm pots once they reach the four leaf stage, when they're a few cm tall.

Starting the seeds off in an airing cupboard can also help them, especially for chilli peppers (I've grown a chilli pepper which required a temperature over 24°C to germinate). Once germinated, they'll be fine on a sunny windowsill. Aubergines may germinate better if you soak the seeds in warm water and leave them for 24 hours before sowing.

Make sure you harden the seedlings off, as discussed above, before you finally move them outside, and feed them once the first fruit has set. (If your potting compost is a bit weak, you may want to feed when you first pot them out, as well. Make sure that the plants don't dry out.) For aubergines, pinch out the top of the plant at about 45cm tall to encourage bushiness, but remove any side shoots once you have three or four fruits set. There should be no need to do this for peppers.

Harvesting

Peppers can be harvested when still green, but they get sweeter as they ripen and change colour. Varieties exist which are red, orange, yellow, or even purple. Aubergines and hot chilli peppers should be harvested only when fully ripe.

Growing Potatoes in Containers

Potatoes are pleasingly easy to grow, and the good news is that they're not only for people with gardens – they can also be grown very successfully in containers. Some gardeners swear by containers for potatoes even if they have access to open ground!

Containers

There are many possible options for housing your container potatoes. A straightforward one is a large pot, the larger the better. However, this is a bit of a waste of space, in that the potatoes will only be in there for a few months (but the pot will always be taking up space); and it can be harder to harvest from a pot. A better option could be a thick heavy duty black plastic sack (punch a couple of holes in the bottom), or a cardboard box (line with a plastic sack – an old compost sack is ideal – with holes punched in the bottom). A stack of tyres is a possibility: use a sharp Stanley knife to cut out the inside part of the tyres, then stack them on top of one another. This, however, like the large pot option, has a fairly large footprint, and unless you put some kind of bottom (a black plastic sack again?) on the base of the tyre stack, you'll end up with a big pile of soil to sweep up at the end of the season. However, tyres can be easy to get hold of if you live anywhere near a garage, so may be cheaper than a pot.

You can also use several smaller buckets – one per tuber. Note that earlies (see below) won't necessarily fill up all the vertical space that you give them, so if sowing earlies you may be better off with smaller containers anyway.

Finding seed potatoes

Once you've found your container, the next thing is to get hold of a couple of seed potatoes. Friends who have allotments may be able to spare some, or you could try just letting a potato from the local farmers' market sprout. It's best not to do this with supermarket potatoes, as you can't be sure that they are pest and disease free. However, growing in pots is less risky for this than growing in open soil, because if you do see signs of disease you can get rid of the contaminated soil afterwards. So if you can't get hold of 'real' seed potatoes, try the supermarket ones.

Definitely do not save seed potatoes from these for use the year after, however. Some garden centres may sell seed potatoes by weight, which is good as you'll only want a couple of them. Garden Organic have in the past done a potato growing day in early January when they sell single seed potatoes from lots of different varieties.

Types of potato

There are four basic types of potato:

1. *First earlies*: can be sown in the south of the UK from mid-March (end of March or early April in the north), and will be ready about 10 weeks later.

2. *Second earlies*: sown around the same time as first earlies, and take around 15 weeks to be ready.

3. *Main crop*: sown a little later (early April in the south of the UK), and take around 18 weeks to be ready.

4. *Late main crop*: sown around the same time as main crop, but take about 20 weeks to be ready.

The main differences are in the time taken to be ready, and the space needed for the potatoes. Main crop and late main crop need more room, but they also store best, so are the potatoes to sow if you have an allotment and want a large crop. In the context of a small urban space, and growing in a container, you'll probably want to grow first or second earlies. Feel free to try main crop if you have a large container, though!

Tiny salad potatoes (usually second earlies) are best grown in a container even if you have access to regular soil, as they're easier to get out of a container than if you sow them in the ground. These may therefore be your best choice for container growing. Otherwise, earlies are another good option.

Chitting, sowing and earthing up

Once you have your potatoes, you need to chit them, which means putting them somewhere warm and light so they can start to sprout. Egg cartons are good for putting potatoes in to chit, or you can line them up in an old pizza box. If you look at the potato, you'll see it has a little dimple

Potato plants first showing their heads, at the bottom of a box lined with a plastic bag.

Potato plants growing well later in the season.

at one end. This is its bottom, from where the roots will sprout. Put that bit downwards, if possible, when chitting. They should be somewhere warm and light. I usually just put mine out on the living room floor near the window, but this may not always be popular with housemates.

Once they've chitted, it's time to sow them out. Easter Sunday is traditional, but a little earlier in March is fine if you're past the risk of frost. Put a few centimetres of stones in the bottom of the container for drainage, then about 15cm of potting compost. Put the potatoes in with their bottoms facing downwards, and cover them over until they're just buried. Unless you're sowing earlies, don't cover right to the top of the container! Just make sure you can't see any of the potato shoots. If you're using a plastic bag, you should fold the bag down to just above the level of the compost; if you're using a tyre stack, you should only have the bottom tyre in place now; if using a bucket or dustbin, don't worry about this. Water well, and leave them to grow (making sure you carry on watering).

Again, you can probably get away with a smaller spacing than is given on the label. Each plant may crop a little less, but you'll have more plants. I got four potato plants in a 12 bottle cardboard wine box, and harvested a couple of handfuls of (very tasty) potatoes from it.

When the shoots start to show above the surface, let them grow a bit, then earth up around them by adding more compost or other organic material. Straw is often recommended, but you can use more or less anything organic. I've found this to be a great way of using shredded paper! You'll need to mix in some compost as well to help thicken it up a bit. Fill up to just below or even just above the level of the top of the shoot (roll up the bag or add another tyre, as necessary), and let it grow a bit more. Keep repeating this process until your container is full all the way to the top, then just let the potatoes grow. You should get potatoes growing all the way down the shoot that you've covered up, which is a great way of using vertical space to maximise your crop. Note, however, that earlies only set potatoes once, so this isn't a useful strategy for them, only for main crop.

Another important way of maximising your crop is to water copiously at the right time, which is when the flowers have just appeared. In general, potatoes need a fair amount of water, but watering heavily at this time is when you'll get the best return for the watering effort. You could also add a little plant food at this point to increase your crop.

Harvesting

After a few weeks, the plants will flower, and you can harvest your first handful of tiny new potatoes. Stick your hand into the soil just around the plants, and see what you can pull up. Take only a couple of potatoes per plant, and leave the rest to get a bit bigger. Boil immediately and eat with a little butter or oil (and some parsley, also from your balcony, see p.76), and appreciate. Potatoes fresh out of the ground are a mindblowingly good experience!

If you want, you can harvest the lot now and get salad potatoes, or you can leave the rest of the potatoes further down to grow a bit bigger, and keep grubbing around every time you fancy a potato or two.

New potatoes fresh from the box.

As in the list above, maincrop potatoes should be ready to eat in 18-20 weeks, by which time the haulms (stalks) will have died down, while earlies are ready sooner.

Potatoes can of course be stored (best results with maincrop potatoes), but you're unlikely to grow enough in a container to worry about this too much. If you aren't using them straight away, though, make sure you put them away dry and keep them somewhere dark.

You can keep a couple of potatoes to use as seed potatoes next year (unless you used supermarket potatoes in the first place). Again, store them somewhere dry until it's time to start chitting them.

Oregano

There are around fifty different types of 'oregano', including sweet marjoram, which is an oregano. *Origanum vulgare* is what is normally meant by 'oregano' when cooking, and it's this that you'll probably want to grow. Having said that, you can also get specific Greek and Italian varieties of oregano (among many others!), so make a decision based on the sort of cooking you do. If you have enough space and use enough oregano to make it worthwhile, you can of course grow more than one variety.

Sweet marjoram is another variety of oregano. Grow it in much the same way as oregano, but note that it is much less likely to survive the winter (you may be successful if you bring it inside), and also that it prefers moister soil than oregano.

Growing

If growing from seed, cover the seeds only very lightly, as oregano seeds require a little light to germinate. It's best to start them indoors if possible, as they'll germinate faster in the warmth, but germination will happen eventually outside as well. Plant out when 5cm tall (harden off first if the seeds were germinated inside), with one plant per 20cm pot. You can also grow oregano from a cutting, in which case the best time to take it is in the summer; or you can grow it from a root division taken in the autumn.

As a Mediterranean herb, oregano wants well-drained, fairly thin soil, and full sun. It can tolerate getting a little dry, and indeed is more likely to struggle if it becomes waterlogged (water a little more copiously for sweet marjoram). It only needs to be fed once or twice in the season, as over-feeding can damage the flavour of the leaves.

Pinch the flowers when they appear to prevent the plant from bolting. If it does bolt, you can save the seeds and resow them the following spring.

Oregano is usually described as a half-hardy annual, meaning that it is unlikely to survive the winter. I've managed to keep oregano going for more than one season, though. If you have a cold frame, it should keep growing even if temperatures drop a little below freezing, and will recover in the spring. Without a cold frame, you may find, if you have a warm microclimate, that it will die back over the winter but regenerate in the spring (as has happened with my plant in the past).

Culinary uses

Oregano will taste best before the plant flowers, and you can start harvesting it when the plants are a few centimetres tall. If you cut stems off at the bottom, you'll encourage the plant to grow more stems and thus to become more bushy (which is probably what you want for cooking purposes). Strip the leaves by holding at the top and running your fingers down the stem.

As a rule, oregano is used as a dried herb. You can dry your own leaves by picking on a dry day and storing them somewhere dry, dark, and warm until they've dried out. Store in an airtight container and use within six months. Sweet marjoram, with its more delicate flavour, may be a better choice if you want to use a fresh herb, and especially in salads; however, I regularly use oregano as a fresh herb and like the taste, so take your pick.

Oregano goes very nicely in Italian dishes and other tomato-based dishes. I often use it together with basil in tomato-based pasta sauces. You can also scatter dried oregano over potatoes when roasting them (rosemary, see p.67).

Medicinal uses

Oregano tea is said to help with a wide range of problems, including indigestion, bloating, coughs, bronchial problems, and headaches. To make an oregano tea, put two tablespoons of fresh herb, or one tablespoon of dried, into a non-metal pot, add a mug's worth of boiling water, and allow to steep for around five minutes. Add honey and/or lemon to taste when you pour.

Marjoram has historically been used for relief of hay fever or sinus congestion symptoms, or coughs and colds. It's calming and mildly antioxidant. Make and drink as a tea in the same way as with oregano.

A handful of dried leaves of either marjoram or oregano in the bath (put in a muslin bag and hang under the tap if you don't want to have to clean damp leaves out of the bath when you're done!) is relaxing and can help soothe tired muscles. Rosemary is also good for aching muscles, so try a sprig of both together.

CHAPTER 6

APRIL

April is another busy month: more sowing, more planting out, and you should be starting to harvest your early veg. It's also a good time to think about companion planting, as the pests are also beginning to wake up.

My Balcony at the Start of April

Plants growing:

Herbs: sage, mint, rosemary, bay, thyme (just starting to grow back), chives, oregano, basil (just moved outside).

Overwintered **peas** (early dwarf and mangetout) beginning to flower.

Overwintered **beans** growing well.

Overwintered **rocket** going to seed.

Overwintered **bronze arrowhead lettuce**.

Small self-seeded **ruby chard**.

Early sowings of **rocket** and **bronze arrowhead lettuce** doing well.

Seeds and cuttings:

Various **tomato** seedlings on the windowsill indoors, waiting to be planted out.

Chilli and **pepper** seeds still germinating.

Basil seeds still germinating.

Tiny **carrot** seedlings.

Microgreens.

Potatoes chitting in a box inside.

Some of my herbs on the herb table in April.

Peas flowering in April.

Things to Do in April

- Sow more lettuces and other greens (succession sowing).
- Sow tomatoes on the windowsill.
- Sow mangetout and other later peas.
- Sow courgettes on the windowsill.
- Sow strawberry seeds.
- Sow potatoes (p.97).
- Sow companion plants – marigolds, nasturtiums, and lavender (p.116).
- Plant out citrus (p.65).
- Herbs: sow fennel (p.151), sage outdoors (p.40), thyme (p.51), parsley indoors (p.76); savory (p.136), basil outdoors after last frost (p.144).
- Take sage cuttings (p.136).
- Start harvesting peas as they appear.
- Keep harvesting the cut-and-come-again overwintered green leafy veg.
- Tie in raspberries or blackberries as the canes grow (p.62).
- Thin seedlings as necessary.
- Make fertiliser (p.119).

Tomatoes

I live far enough south, especially given my south-facing, concrete backed balcony and consequent very warm microclimate, that I can start my tomatoes off in March and plant them out in early April if the weather is behaving as usual. For most people, you won't want to start them off until early April, and then plant out in late April or early May if further north. Bear in mind that tomatoes are delicate and that if you plant them out too early, their progress will be paused if it gets too cold. It's better to wait until it's definitely warm enough for them outside. However, starting them as early as possible is a good idea, to give them plenty of time to crop and ripen. One year I wasn't able to start mine until July, and most of my crop was green (see p.37 for a recipe for green tomatoes).

There are a huge number of varieties of tomatoes, but they fall into two basic categories:

1. **Vine** or **Indeterminate** varieties. These are the most commonly-grown types. They need support from a cane, cage, or a piece of string hung from a fence (the option I often use), as the vines can grow quite long and won't support their own weight. Left to their own devices they'll just keep growing until it gets too cold and they die off, which means that after a certain number of trusses of fruit have appeared, you need to pinch out the growing tip to encourage the fruit to ripen. You also need to pinch out side shoots (see p.110) to grow more fruit and less foliage. They work great in pots.

2. **Bush** or **Determinate** varieties. These flower and then set fruit all at once, at the end of each branch, which means they don't need to have their side shoots removed, or the growing tip pinched out (once they've set fruit, they stop growing). They don't need much support, but they do take up more room so may be less use in containers. You can also get dwarf bush varieties which are bred for hanging baskets and work well in containers.

There are also different types of fruit from both categories. The best known are cherry tomatoes (small tomatoes), standard tomatoes (as the name suggests, 'normal' tomatoes), beefsteak tomatoes (larger than standard ones), and plum tomatoes (oval, firm, and freeze well). In small spaces your best bet is probably to focus on cherry tomatoes.

Note: if you want to be able to seed save, make sure you buy heritage rather than hybrid tomatoes. See p.56 for more on seed saving and other options for getting hold of seeds.

Sowing

Sow tomato seeds either one to a small seed plug, or a couple to a slightly larger pot. Different varieties will take different lengths of time to germinate, but 1-2 weeks is normal. Make sure you label the varieties when you're sowing so later on you will know which varieties worked best for you. Once you have ripened fruit, you can very easily seed save from the plants that worked best (see p.56 for more on seed saving), as tomatoes breed true. Even if that doesn't work, it's good to be able to buy your preferred variety again.

Ripe cherry tomatoes in late summer – note the string supporting the vine-type plant.

Planting out

Once the seedlings have a couple of real leaves and are 7.5-10cm high, you should either move them into a bigger pot, or plant them out into the pot they'll eventually stay in. I prefer to replant them twice (once into a larger pot, once into their final home). The main advantage of this is that each time, you can bury a bit more of the stem. Those tiny hairs on the stem will become

Tomato seedlings on the windowsill, nearly ready to plant out.

Tomatoes in their second pots outside.

roots if they're underground, giving the plant a better anchor in the earth. This is true for all nightshades (tomatoes, peppers, aubergines, potatoes, etc).

By the time the plant is 15cm or so tall, it's time to replant it into its final pot. This should be at least 30cm across, and fairly deep. Tomatoes do particularly well in self-watering containers (see p.73), as they need a lot of water. A self-watering container will help ensure that they don't dry out and thus wilt. Even if you give it a drink after it's wilted and thus revitalise it, the plant will experience a shock each time this happens, which may stunt its growth and production.

When planting out tomatoes (or any other plant), be careful with the plant's roots as you take it out of the pot, and make sure you leave enough space in the new pot to get the roots in with plenty of room. See p.82 for a longer discussion of planting out.

Another useful tip for tomatoes is to bury a little crushed eggshell underneath them when you plant them into their final container. The extra protein in the eggshell helps to feed them, and the calcium helps to prevent blossom-end rot. A quick feed (see p.119 for potential fertilisers) when watering in after you've planted them out is also a good idea, and you should keep feeding regularly throughout the growing season.

Planting out a tomato plant into a self-watering container.

You may well find that you have too many seedlings, if all of them have grown properly. It always seems a shame just to throw them away; you can try to offload them on to friends (a tomato plant is a great introduction to food growing in containers), or you can experiment with guerrilla tomato gardening! (See p.188.)

Care and feeding

For vine tomatoes, you'll need to provide some kind of support. Either tie the main shoot, and any other side shoots that start to sag, up with a piece of string suspended from something higher up, or go for the more traditional approach of using a cane or two, or a tomato cage.

If you do use canes, put a cork or something similar on the top of them to avoid the potential of an eye injury.

Tomatoes need quite a bit of fertiliser to do well – they're quite greedy, and regular feeding can make a big difference to the output you get. You should be feeding them every week or so during the main growing season. (see p.119 for a discussion on fertilisers). If you didn't put eggshell under them when you planted them, try to use a fertiliser with some calcium in to minimise the chances of blossom-end rot.

Even more important is to keep watering the plants copiously. As long as your pots have drainage holes, it's really pretty hard to overwater tomatoes. Insufficient water will put stress on the plants and reduce your crop; and can even lead to diseases.

This sideshoot just appearing is easy to pinch out. See next page.

This sideshoot should have been pinched out some time ago and is now as big as the other branches. See next page.

My best tomato this year was a vine variety, planted in a self-watering container and trained up a south-facing wall.

The other thing to consider is whether you pinch them out. This is only necessary for vine varieties; bush varieties don't need pinching out (tomato varieties are discussed on p.106). If you leave vine (also known as 'indeterminate') tomato plants to their own devices, a stem will start to grow from each 'joint' between the main stem and it branches. These side shoots will tend to produce a lot of foliage but not so many tomatoes. If you pinch them out when they appear, the plant concentrates its energy into producing fruit, which is of course what we want.

When the plant has six or seven batches of fruit setting (these are known as trusses), pinch out the growing tip (i.e. the top of the plant, where it's still growing upwards), to encourage it to put energy into the existing fruit. Without this, you may wind up with a lot of lower quality fruit that doesn't ripen in time before the end of the season.

Having said that, if you're already getting good quality fruit that's ripening happily, you may want to experiment with letting the plant set a few more fruit, and see what happens. I'm a great fan of trying different things out to see what gives you the sort of success *you* want.

See p.159 for a recipe for ripe tomatoes, and p.37 for what to do with any green tomatoes left over at the end of the season.

Courgettes

Courgettes are pretty easy to grow. They need fertiliser and quite a lot of water, but once they're established, if you keep providing these, they can be very productive. However, if you're only growing a single plant, or don't have much insect life in your space (for example if you have a high-up balcony), you may have problems with pollination. This is discussed further below.

You can get courgette plants whose fruit comes in a variety of different shapes. Whilst most courgettes are the regular long sort, you can also get ball courgettes, and yellow and white varieties (my experience is that the yellow ones are less tasty, but they do look pretty).

Courgette plants come in either bush or vine type, although the majority are bushes. For growing in a pot, you want a bush type, and you should go for a reasonably compact variety. Real Seeds do a 'Verde di Milano' variety which is a small plant (and which I had great success with this year in the allotment, but sadly not in a container), and if you want an F1 Hybrid, try Midnight, which is compact and bushy. If you're concerned about pollination (see below), you can also try Cavili F1, which doesn't require pollination to set fruit. I haven't personally tried this so can't comment further; and being an F1 hybrid, it also has the problem that you can't save seed from it.

Sowing

Courgettes are another vegetable that are best started off inside to give them a chance to get going as early as possible. The seeds are big enough (and the plants get large quickly enough) that you want one seed per little pot. They should take around 1-2 weeks to germinate, although I have found that sometimes they'll take longer, particularly if it's been a little cold (even if sown indoors). Don't give up hope! You can speed up germination by using a propagator, or just by covering the pots in clingfilm. Be sure to take the clingfilm off once the seeds have sprouted, so that the plants can breathe.

Courgette flowers just starting to appear. You can already see that some of them have the beginnings of fruit behind them.

This courgette wasn't fertilised, and is already starting to look a bit sorry for itself at its base.

You shouldn't plant courgettes out until after the last frost date, as they're very susceptible to the cold. When the plants have produced their first proper leaves, you can move them into a larger pot and start hardening them off. Then after a week or so of hardening off, plant them out into a pot at least 30cm across.

Make sure the compost is fertile and feed the plants regularly (about weekly) while they're growing.

Fertilising courgettes for fruit

Eventually, you'll start seeing flowers on your plants. Courgettes grow both male and female flowers on the same plant. The female flowers are the ones that produce the fruit, but they need to be fertilised by a male flower in order for the fruit to grow properly.

The male flowers are the ones that have only a stalk behind them, and the female ones have the start of a tiny fruit. Once the female flower is fertilised, the baby courgette will grow into a full-size courgette; if it doesn't get fertilised, the baby courgette will fail to fill out properly, and eventually will rot away and fall off.

Although each plant has both male and female flowers, they can't always self-fertilise. If you're growing courgettes on the ground and you have several of them, insects will do the cross-fertilising for you, so there's no need for action on your part. If you're growing only one or two courgette plants and you're off the ground, or otherwise don't have many insects around the place, you may need to do the fertilisation yourself.

Wait until a female flower is open. You might need to check on them early in the morning if you have trouble finding them open, but don't force them open, as in this case they won't be ready to pollinate and it won't work. Then pick a male flower, strip its petals off, and gently push it into the female flower. Alternatively, you can use a thin paintbrush or a cotton bud: dip the paintbrush into the male flower and collect a little pollen on it, then shake or dab the pollen into the female flower. If it's a windy day, it may be worth closing the female flower up with a rubber band afterwards, to make sure that the pollen does its job.

You can either do this as soon as your female flowers start to appear, on the assumption that you'll have problems, or wait to see if your courgettes manage to do the job by themselves. From my own experience, I'd recommend assuming that you'll need to help the plant out if you're growing on a balcony and if you have only a single plant. However, if you've grown insect attracting flowers (see p.116 for discussion of companion planting and attracting insects) you may be able to get away without it. Note that if the weather's cool, you may only get male flowers at first. Be patient! The female flowers will follow in due course, and courgette plants last for quite a while, and will keep growing for as long as you keep picking the plants.

Keep an eye on your growing baby courgettes – they can go very quickly from 'a bit too small' to 'enormous monsters'. Pick regularly, since picking fruit encourages the plant to produce more.

Eating courgettes

Courgettes are lovely fried quickly with a little garlic, or eaten in pasta sauce. Make sure you pick them fairly early – if you leave them a day or two too late, they suddenly turn into enormous marrow-type things and taste far less good.

You can also deep fry and eat the male courgette flowers. It's a delicate flavour, but worth the effort at least once or twice, especially given how pretty they are. It also means that even if you have trouble getting the female flowers fertilised, you'll get something edible from the experience.

Strawberries

This isn't the right time of year to propagate strawberries – that should be done in July (see p.148). However, if you do come across a spare strawberry plant (this year I wound up with a few rogue ones from my allotment that hadn't been picked up in the autumn), put it into a trough or hanging basket and water it in well. You can also buy plants from garden centres at this time of year to be planted out after the first frost.

There are two basic types of strawberries: regular strawberries, of the sort you see in shops, and Alpine strawberries, which are rather closer to wild strawberries, and which are small and very intensely flavoured. Either type is perfectly amenable to being grown in a pot.

Sowing

In general, strawberries are grown from runners from established plants rather than from seeds. A friend with a strawberry patch is a good source of these, in early autumn (see p.148 for more on propagating strawberries). But Alpine or wild strawberries can be successfully grown from seed, and now is a good time of year to sow those. Either start them inside, or wait till after the first frost. If you put the seed in the freezer for a couple of weeks before sowing, it will help to jump start them.

When sowing seeds, use a seed tray with half an inch of compost, sprinkle the seeds over it, and add a light dusting of compost on top. The seeds should be covered, but not thickly. Keep the seeds moist and in direct sunlight, and expect to wait 2-3 weeks for germination.

Planting out

Once the third leaves have appeared, plant them out into larger pots. If it's warm enough by now, you can plant them outside. A hanging basket or trough is a good pot to use, as strawberries have quite shallow roots.

Water your suckers or seedlings plentifully at first, then once the plants are established, only when the soil is dry. Fertilise monthly, and every 10 days during the growing season.

For plants grown from seed, you shouldn't let the flowers set fruit in the first year. If you see any flowers, pick them off the plant. This makes sure that the plant is established before it produces fruit, and will mean that you get more fruit next year. Otherwise, it may wear itself out too early.

Care and cropping

Strawberries are usually ready to harvest in June. They tend to ripen over a period of time, rather than all at once, so you'll get a few strawberries a day, rather than a large batch on one day. Happily, they're far nicer eaten this way than the all approximately ripe boxes you buy from the supermarket!

Once the fruit start to grow, and certainly as they start to ripen, you may run into problems with slugs. See p.133 for more discussion about dealing with slugs, but putting copper tape around the trough or pot that they're in may help.

Making the Most of Your Space (Reprise)

Hopefully, you started off with a reasonable plan to make the best use of your space (p.15). However, as the pots begin to stack up at this time of year, you may find that it isn't working out quite as you imagined. Don't hesitate to rearrange a bit! Nothing is set in stone, and one of the advantages of growing in pots is that you *can* rearrange things very easily.

It can also be useful to move plants around at different stages of their life. For example, the tomato seedlings may do better up on a windowsill off the ground when they're first planted out, whereas later on they can be moved to somewhere else. Some plants may want the most sunshine at particular points of time. Your peas will be finished cropping in late May, and you can move their pots somewhere else (and sow something else in them) and move the tomatoes up to use the vines that the peas were growing up, or sow French bean seedlings in their place instead. Experiment, and make sure that you keep notes!

Companion Planting

There are two main reasons to use flowers as companion plants: to discourage pests, and to encourage beneficial insects. Plenty of plants need insects to fertilise them; and it's also good to encourage insects in the environment, as cities can be inhospitable to them.

Obviously, in a container garden, you have limited space, but it's still worth giving up some of that space to flowers. Even better, you can choose flowers that have multiple uses, and that can also be eaten or used medicinally.

Marigolds

Marigolds (pot marigolds, or *Calendula officinalis*) are easy to grow from seed. They're an annual, so you'll need to resow every year, but they grow extremely easily, and given half a chance will reseed themselves. Cut off the dead flower heads as soon as they expire to encourage new growth, and you should keep getting new flowers through till the autumn. (Although if you want them to self-seed, you'll need to leave some dead heads to go to seed, perhaps later in the season.)

Sow in March or April directly into the pot or container that you want them in, and thin to aabout 5cm apart when the seedlings appear. You can also make a late sowing at the end of August to get plants that will overwinter and flower early in the next spring.

They're a great pest repellent, with a very strong smell. Sow them either in containers alongside your veg containers, or put a couple of seeds in the pot with plants that you're concerned about pests on.

Marigolds are edible: the flowers and petals make a pretty garnish, and can also be used in soups, salads, and rice dishes. They're slightly bitter, with an aromatic flavour.

They're also medicinally useful. Research has found that calendula is an antiseptic and anti-inflammatory (thus supporting its historic use for wounds and ulcers!), and can also be used to treat some fungal infections including athlete's foot and candida. To make up an oil, dry some flowers thoroughly (to avoid making the oil bad), put the dried flowers in a clean glass jar, and cover with olive oil or rape seed oil. Close the jar and leave in a sunny place for about three weeks. Filter the oil into another container through a muslin cloth to remove the flowers, then pour it through a funnel into a dark bottle and stopper tightly. You can apply this oil to minor wounds, varicose veins, sunburn, and other similar afflictions.

Marigold tea is recommended for a sore throat. Put a teaspoon of dried or a couple of teaspoons of fresh flowers into a teapot, pour boiling water over it, and leave to infuse for 5-10 minutes. Drink with a little honey to taste.

Nasturtiums

Nasturtiums are another self-seeding annual, and again, are easy to grow. Nasturtiums deter aphids, so sow them among your rocket and lettuce.

The leaves, flowers, and seeds of nasturtiums are all edible. The leaves taste rather like watercress – quite peppery – and can be added to salads, egg dishes, cheese dishes, and so on. You can use the flowers as an edible gar-

nish, much like marigolds, or chop them and add them to olive oil as a pasta topping.

Nasturtium seeds can be substituted for capers, if you pick them young (when still green and soft). Put one cup of rinsed and drained nasturtium seeds into a clean 500ml jar, then bring a cup of vinegar, a teaspoon of salt, and a little pepper to the boil. Pour the vinegar, salt, and pepper into the jar over the seed pods, seal and label the jar, and leave in the fridge for 3 months before eating. You can add extra spices or herbs to the vinegar if you like (try thyme or crushed garlic).

You can also make a nasturtium vinegar which has a nice flavour. Simply add around a dozen rinsed and dried flowers to a cup of white wine vinegar in a glass jar with a screw lid, and let steep for 1-3 weeks. (Note: if the jar lid is metal, line it with plastic to avoid the vinegar discolouring it.) Strain and put into an appropriate bottle.

Lavender

Lavender repels a couple of pests, but its advantage is primarily in encouraging beneficial insects. A small pot of lavender on the edge of your balcony will act to draw insects in.

Lavender will grow from seed in the spring. Start the seeds off somewhere warm, around 6-8 weeks before your last frost date. They can take up to a month to germinate. Transplant to 5cm pots once they have a couple of sets of true leaves. Once they're around 7.5cm tall, harden them off by leaving them outside for a little longer each day over a week, then plant them out into a pot at least 30cm big. Larger pots will lead to larger lavender.

Alternatively, you can start lavender from a cutting taken in the summer (between June and September). Pull a non-flowering side shoot off from the main stem, with a little strip of bark attached (this is where the new roots will develop). Remove enough lower leaves to give a bare stem, dip the end of the cutting into rooting hormone if you have any (or use willow bark infusion, as discussed on p.52), and insert it into a small pot of compost. It's a good idea to take several cuttings, to ensure that at least one takes successfully. Water in well, then cover the pot with the top of a plastic water bottle or a clear plastic sandwich bag, to keep the cuttings moist and humid. Place in a warm, shaded place, and after a couple of weeks, cut the corner of the bag off, removing it altogether after a couple more weeks. Pot the cuttings individually once they're well-established.

Alternatively, you can take the more kamikaze attitude of just putting them into pots of compost outside, and hoping for the best. I haven't propagated lavender this way, but I have successfully propagated mint, sage, and rosemary with minimal effort and attention. If doing this, definitely start a number of cuttings off, as it's a bit kill-or-cure.

Cut off any flowering stems in the first season to allow the plant to gain strength.

As well as its companion plant properties, lavender also has many medicinal uses. Put dried lavender in a pillow to encourage sleep.

It can also be used in food. Lavender flowers are edible, and are nice in salads, or as part of a stew or wine-based sauce. They are nice in sweet dishes (for example, as a garnish for ice cream), or you can make lavender sugar by putting a couple of lavender flowers in a sugar container for a few weeks. Lavender's subtle flavour is well worth experimenting with; start with a little at a time and see how you get on.

Fertiliser

As discussed on p.80, if you're using old compost, you'll definitely need to feed all of your plants at least once (even Mediterranean herbs can probably use a little food). Even if you have fresh compost, most vegetables could use a little food to help produce a better crop, and if you're growing plants like tomatoes, peppers, and courgettes, you'll need to feed rather more often.

The basic permaculture approach to soil fertility is to add more organic matter, and that's a good basic approach whether you're growing in the ground or in containers. However, in containers, you don't have any soil life generating fertility for you; you have to put it all in yourself. You're also slightly more limited in the options you can use; green manures and dynamic accumulators (such as comfrey) are a less useful option in a limited space. (Dynamic accumulators are plants which are particularly good at mining nutrients from the soil with their roots, and which can then be used as a fertiliser. Unfortunately, they're of little use in containers.)

Worm compost is very rich, and mixing in a little worm compost with the potting compost when you put plants in pots is a good way of feeding by adding organic matter; unfortunately, unlike in an allotment where there are worms and other creatures living in the soil, just putting extra compost on the top of the soil won't help nutrients reach the plant roots. You'll need to mix it in, or use liquid fertiliser. Worm tea – the liquid that comes out of the bottom of your wormery – is an excellent liquid fertiliser and great for perking up drooping seedlings.

A quick and easy liquid food option is to buy organic container plant food online or in a garden centre. However, for a cheaper and more sustainable option, you can make your own. Nettles and comfrey are both useful for feeding purposes, and you can even use the very readily available substance, human urine!

119

Fertilisers should contain at least one of the three major plant food elements:

- Nitrogen (N): for stem and leaf growth.
- Phosphate (P): for root growth.
- Potassium (K): for flower and fruit production.

You will want a fertiliser with more of one or the other depending on the time of year and the type of plant. For example, you want plenty of N for your spinach to encourage leaf growth, and for your tomatoes and peppers at the start of the season to get the stems and leaves growing; but later in the season those same tomatoes will want plenty of K to encourage fruit production. Multipurpose fertilisers have some of all three elements, which is fine.

Nettles

Nettles are usually pretty easy to find in urban parks or patches of waste ground. You want to harvest them in early to mid spring, before they flower. Be careful where you get them from: avoid areas which are very close to heavy traffic, for example, as the plants will have picked up a lot of air pollution. Don't over-harvest: leave some nettles behind to set flowers. (Although nettles are fairly hard to get rid of, so you don't need to be too careful.)

For fertiliser, you can pick the whole plant (for nettle soup, just use the tops of the plants). Use gloves to avoid being stung! Get about a carrier bag full of nettles, then take them home, put them into a bucket

or other container with a weight on top of them, cover them with water, and cover the bucket. If it's easier, you can use a smaller container – I used a couple of large jars. However, if using jars, don't seal them properly, and don't leave them in the sunshine, or the nettles will ferment a little too fast and overflow the jar.

Leave the whole thing for a couple of weeks, then fish out the nettles and dump them into the compost. Dilute the remaining nettle 'tea' about 1:10 with water, and water your plants. Nettle tea is high in N so is good to encourage strong leafy growth. Be careful not to get it on the leaves as it can burn them.

Be warned: it smells pretty vile. Avoid getting it on your shoes or clothes as the smell will linger for a long time!

Since it's best to pick nettles before they flower, you may want to make a large quantity of this in the spring and keep some of it for later in the season.

Comfrey

Comfrey is a little harder to come by than nettles, but you can sometimes find it growing wild, or if you know someone with an allotment, they may be able to spare you a few leaves. It's less painful to harvest than nettles, but it can be a bit scratchy, so again it's best to wear gloves. Take a few leaves, or chop off the tops of the plants. Comfrey is pretty tough, so there's little need to worry about over-harvesting, but as always with wild foraging, don't take the whole plant.

Comfrey tea is made in much the same way as nettle tea, and unfortunately smells just about as bad. Again, after a couple of weeks of steeping the leaves in water, fish them out and put them in the compost bin, and use the comfrey tea diluted 1:10 with water to feed your plants.

A less smelly version of comfrey tea can be made by putting comfrey leaves into a black plastic container, compressing them right down (perhaps with a brick on top), and covering them. Do not add extra water; just leave them to rot down. Eventually you'll get a thick sludgy liquid, which you can dilute and use as liquid fertiliser. Multiple applications of a weak dilution are better for the plant than a single strong application.

Comfrey tea is fairly high in K (which it extracts from deep in the soil via its long roots), so it's good for the fruit and flower growing stage of the season.

Comfrey can be picked all through the summer, so if you can

find a source of comfrey, it's a good option to use later in the season once it's too late for nettles.

How to stop liquid manure smelling

There are, however, ways of minimising smell. Give the mixture a stir each day to mix oxygen into the liquid. This also helps the survival of the bacteria breaking down the plants. The mixture will produce big bubbles on the surface which means the fermenting process is happening. You need to keep an eye on this as when it has finished bubbling you can strain the liquid through a net to get the majority of the plant material out. Finally, pass the liquid through an old kitchen sieve.

The fermentation process can take anything from 10 days to 3 weeks, depending on the temperature. The warmer it is, the quicker the process. To further minimise the smell, you can also put a few drops of valerian or other essential oils or a handful of rosemary and thyme into the mix.

Urine

Many people are a little put off by this idea, which is fair enough; and you do need to be a little careful with it. However, human urine is environmentally friendly, extremely beneficial, and safe to use on plants as it's sterile. It's very high in N, and a Finnish study found that it increased yields by up to 4 times. You'll also save water by flushing the toilet that bit less often.

NOTE: do not use urine if you have a urinary tract infection or similar. If you're on significant medication or the contraceptive pill, you may also want to avoid it (over-the-counter vitamins or pills are unlikely to be problematic, especially as you'll be applying it dilute).

Dilute the urine at around 1:30 with water, and apply directly to the soil. Try to avoid getting it onto the leaves, as the high N level means that you can 'burn' the leaves. Avoid using urine fertiliser on food plants for a couple of weeks before harvesting, and it's best not to use this on plants whose leaves you are harvesting on a regular basis. You're probably OK to use it on peas or beans if you're careful to water at the base of the plant, and you can certainly use it in the early growth stages of tomatoes, peppers, courgettes, potatoes, and so on.

Urine should be used within 24 hours if you're putting it straight onto plants. If it's older than this it can be added to a regular compost heap, but don't add it to a worm compost bin.

Compost tea

If you have the time and inclination, you can make compost tea, which is one way of making a little compost go a lot further. It's not strictly speaking a fertiliser, but a way of multiplying beneficial micro-organisms in the soil, benefiting both plants and soil. It is however a little more work than the liquid fertilisers discussed above.

You'll need an aquarium pump and some plastic hose, some worm compost, a couple of buckets, and organic unsulfured black molasses (black treacle). The aquarium pump is used because the sort of tea that's best is aerobic tea, with oxygen in it. This maximises the beneficial organisms, which are largely aerobic. The molasses provides food for these organisms to reproduce.

Start off with a bucket of water and run the pump and hose in it for an hour or so, to dechlorinate the water (you'll need to weight the hose down to keep it at the bottom). Alternatively, just leave it to stand for 24 hours and stir it a few times.

Then get your second bucket, dump a few big handfuls of compost in it (don't pack it down). Weight the hose down so it'll stay under the compost, top the bucket up nearly to the top with your dechlorinated water, then add 2-3 big tablespoons of molasses and stir vigorously. You can also add some seaweed extract if you have it available. Then leave for 24-48 hours, with the bubblers going, to brew.

You need to use the tea as soon as it's done aerating (certainly within 12 hours), otherwise the beneficial aerobic microorganisms will die off. Strain out the solids (and return them to the compost, or put them into your soil), and use the liquid either to revitalise the soil, or as a leaf spray.

Chives

Growing

Chives are an allium, a member of the garlic and onion family. They're easy to grow from seed, and indeed will self-seed given half the chance. Sow the seeds (indoors or outdoors) in early spring, and wait for them to show their heads.

Alternatively, you can grow them from divisions; in early spring or mid-autumn, dig up an established clump of chives, and pull a clump of a few bulbs away from it. Transplant elsewhere and water in well.

Chives are a perennial; they'll die back altogether in the winter, then reappear in the spring. One of my favourite early signs of spring is the new chives starting to appear.

Care

They're extremely easy to look after, and really just need to be watered (reasonably frequently). They like full sun.

They'll flower in late spring or early summer, and after the flowers have dried, you can remove and harvest the little black seeds from between the dried flower petals. As chives are perennial, you probably won't need these yourself, but you can always pass them on to someone else, or grow small pots of chives as presents.

In theory, you should pull up and divide the little clump of bulbs every couple of years. In practice I confess that I've never done this, and my pot of chives has been going strong for about seven years.

Flowering chives in early summer.

One warning: chives and peas don't get on together, so keep the pots apart.

Culinary uses

One of the nicest ways to use chives is in order to add a bit of a bite to a salad, perhaps a salad of other green leaves from your pots! Chives are also nice in scrambled eggs or scrambled tofu, or sprinkled on top of other egg dishes. You can also chop them and sprinkle them on rice, baked potatoes, sandwiches, or any other food. Chives are good in butter or cream cheese. You can dry chives and keep them for later use, but they're better fresh!

Medicinal uses

The main traditional use of chives is to promote appetite or to aid digestion. All alliums (chives, onions, garlic, leeks) contain certain compounds that are believed to help combat hypertension (high blood pressure). Eat the leaves, or make an infusion by pouring boiling water over a couple of tablespoons of chives. Chives are also rich in Vitamin A and Vitamin C when eaten raw.

CHAPTER 7

MAY

By May, any local pests that you might suffer from (ants, aphids, slugs, and so on) are back in action, so you might need to think about ways of dealing with them (or just learn to live with them). This is also the time of year when you're most likely to be overrun with seedlings and looking for homes for them – have you considered a little guerrilla gardening to spread the gardening love a little?

My Balcony at the Start of May

Plants and seedlings:

> **Herbs**: sage, mint, rosemary, bay, thyme, chives, oregano, basil, parsley.

> **Peas** and **beans** growing nicely up their poles; **mangetout** beginning to grow.

> Pot of **microgreens** turning into macrogreens.

> **Bronze arrowhead lettuce**.

> **Ruby chard**.

> **Tomato** seedlings, both inside on the window ledge and outside in pots.

> Two **pepper** seedlings inside on the window ledge.

> **Carrot** seedlings.

> **Potatoes**.

Seeds and cuttings:

> **Courgette** seeds inside on the windowsill.

> **Dill** seeds outside.

Second batch of **carrot** seed outside.

More **rocket** and **mispoona** seeds just starting to germinate.

Alpine **strawberry** seeds – no sign of life yet.

Marigold and **nasturtium** seeds scattered throughout various pots.

Miscellaneous other:

- Worms producing plenty of compost.

Things to Do in May

- Sow microgreens (p.128).

- Continue succession sowing any green leafy veg you're growing.

- Plant out tomatoes into their final pots (p.107).

- Plant out peppers (p.94).

- Sow parsley (p.75) and fennel (p.151) outside.

- Thin plants as necessary.

Microgreens and Baby Greens

Microgreens are the first few small leaves of lettuce, rocket, and similar green leafy plants, harvested when they're only 2.5cm or so high. Baby greens are the same plants a couple of weeks later, when they're maybe 7.5 to 10cm. After that, they turn into grown-up vegetables. Happily, they're edible all the way through this process, so if you miss the boat for harvesting them as microgreens, you can still eat them a bit bigger!

Microgreens are ideal for growing in small or shallow pots or in small spaces, because they don't have much in the way of a root system and they need very little space between plants (as you'll harvest them when they're still very small). This means that you can grow them in quite shallow trays, and fit them into whatever corner you have available – a windowsill or outside. You can use empty plastic packaging – the sort of plastic pot that tomatoes or grapes come in is ideal. These cartons won't last long as the plastic is quite weak, but they'll certainly do at least one batch of greens. Punch five or six drainage holes in the bottom, fill with compost to an inch or so below the top, and use the lid of the package as a drip tray.

Baby greens in a pot that I later planted a tomato into.

Alternatively, if you have pots hanging around waiting for something else (e.g. tomatoes, peppers, courgettes, or anything else that needs a warmer time of year before being planted out), you can grow a crop of microgreens while you're waiting for the weather to improve. Once the bigger plant is ready to go in, either harvest anything that's left, or clear a space in the middle of the pot and keep growing the greens around the edges. I've also grown microgreens in the space around pea plants.

The small quantity of space taken up by a tray of microgreens also means that they're great for keeping a supply of greens growing during the winter on a windowsill (see p.58).

What and how to sow

Which seeds to grow depends on what you prefer to eat. A good idea is to sow a mix of different leaves that go well together. Cress, mustard, radish, and rocket (which comes in various different forms, all of which are tasty in different ways!) are all quite spicy, so you could mix up a bag of those seeds, sow them all together, then harvest them together. Mizuna, kale, and various sorts of lettuce are milder, so you could mix up a separate bag of those seeds for another set of trays. As a rule I just use whatever seeds I have hanging around – usually a mixture of rocket, pak choi, bronze arrowhead lettuce, and mispoona or mizuna.

Whatever you use, sow the seeds fairly thickly (they won't get big enough to worry about overcrowding) and scatter a thin layer of soil over them. Water in well.

Care and harvesting

Keep the soil moist, but not too wet while the seeds are germinating. The first set of leaves you'll see when the seeds start to germinate are called the 'seed leaves'; the earliest you should harvest your microgreens is when the next set of leaves, the first 'true leaves', grow. Snip them off with a pair of scissors (to avoid disturbing the other shoots around them) and eat.

Unfortunately, microgreens aren't cut-and-come-again, as they're effectively just sprouts at this stage, rather than 'real' plants. To extend their lifespan a bit, you can leave some of the plants to grow a little bigger, for example, harvesting every other plant as a microgreen, and then harvest what's left as baby leaves. Note that if you're growing them in a shallow tray, you won't be able to leave them much longer than this, as they'll need more room for their roots as they grow, and will tend to bolt. Keep a close eye on them and be ready to harvest them – in warm weather in particular they grow very quickly! Also, the bigger they get, the more water they need.

If you don't harvest regularly, the plants will bolt rapidly, especially if you've sown thickly and in a shallow tray. Make sure you keep an eye on the plants and are prepared to eat a handful or two of leaves on a daily basis.

The easiest way to keep your supply going is to succession sow: just sow another tray every week or so. As a rule, microgreens take a couple of weeks to germinate and a couple of weeks to grow. In the winter, both stages may be longer (sometimes much longer, depending on where the plants are and how warm your house or windowsill is). Once you've harvested one tray, as long as there were no signs of disease in the plants, you can reuse soil and tray for the next batch (yank out all the old roots first); so once you've got started, you can keep a supply going for as long as you remember to keep sowing.

Unfortunately, you won't be able to seed save, because you're eating your plants before they get anywhere near the flowering and seed setting stage. You can either just keep buying seeds, or move a couple of plants to a full size pot elsewhere and allow them to run to seed in due course (the cheaper and more sustainable option). A couple of rocket plants allowed to run to seed should produce more than enough seed for the next season. See p.56 for more on seed saving for lettuces.

Pests

You're not the only one who's keen to eat the plants that you're growing. There are plenty of other beasts out there that are also eyeing up your crops, and are happy to compete for them. You're likely to suffer slightly less from pests when container gardening, but anything airborne (except carrot fly, which sticks close to the ground) is potentially capable of making its way even to a high balcony, and if you're growing on a patio, even low level pests are likely to be around.

If at all possible, the ideal solution is just to live with them. If you're only losing a few leaves here and there, see if you can simply tolerate that, rather than waging war on insect life. You're highly unlikely to win in the long run, even if you're prepared to use the full chemical arsenal available to the modern gardener and abandon the idea of organic growing. Insect life is also beneficial to the overall ecosystem of the garden.

However, if it really is a bit too much, here are some (organic) tips to redress the balance.

Aphids, also known as greenfly or blackfly (these are different aphid species, but the differences aren't important for our purposes) can be a big problem for gardeners. This is particularly true if you have an ant colony in the area, as the ants will sometimes 'farm' the aphids, protecting them from predators and encouraging them towards the juiciest plants, then 'milking' the aphids for the honeydew they produce. This is impressive behaviour on the part of the ants, but irritating for human gardeners! If this happens, you'll wind up with far more aphids than you would normally expect, and the concentration may be enough to kill the plant. (For discussion of dealing with ants, see below.)

What aphids actually do is to settle on the plant and suck the sap from it, which damages and weakens the plant. It also distorts the leaves, which makes it difficult to spray them (see below) as the aphids are protected by the curl of the leaves. In theory, aphids won't actually kill a plant, but if the infestation is bad enough, such as when the ants get involved, it can weaken the plant enough that it does die.

In my experience, the most popular plants if you're an aphid are broad beans, mizuna, and rocket. Other lettuces can also fall victim, but they do seem particularly enthusiastic about rocket, especially once it's gone to seed. Chard, once flowering, is also popular. My own favourite lettuce variety is bronze arrowhead and my local aphids seem (much to my pleasure) to be entirely uninterested in it; so if you do have problems, it may be worth experimenting to see what is and isn't high on the local aphid preferred food menu.

As a rule, an excess of aphids indicates that there's something not quite right in the local ecosystem. This is all very well in a garden or allotment, where you might expect a fairly varied ecosystem and where you have more scope to encourage other insects, but if you're using a small balcony or roof it may be harder to deal with the problem by rebalancing the ecosystem. There are however still some possible steps to take to encourage natural predators.

You can encourage **ladybirds** by constructing a bug box (see below), by buying ladybird attractant sprays, or by sowing plants that ladybirds like. These include fennel, dill, and coriander – all also useful herbs! – and scented geraniums. However, this is a fairly long-term strategy; and you need to remember that while ladybirds may control aphid populations, they won't actually get rid of them.

Lacewings, wasps, and hoverfly larvae also eat aphids. You may not want to encourage wasps (although it's good to know that they do have a useful purpose in life), but you could consider encouraging lacewings and hoverflies. **Lacewings** like plants that are rich in pollen and nectar, such as rosemary, comfrey (also useful for feeding your plants, see p.121), thyme, mint, and sage. **Hoverflies** like marigolds and nasturtiums (see p.117). These plants are also useful for other reasons, so are a good choice for a limited space. Bees will of course also be encouraged by all nectar-rich flowers, which is good news for all sorts of reasons. See p.116 for more on the advantages of companion planting.

All of these insects are also good to encourage for pollinating plants that require it (such as courgettes). Bug boxes can also provide shelter for endangered insect species such as stag beetles. Again, though, whilst encouraging these beneficial insects will help things back into balance, you'll need to learn to live with a small population of aphids, or there will be no food left for the good insects! It's about finding, as far as possible, a sustainable balance.

There are also short-term solutions available if you have only a small number of aphids. The most common is to spray them with a mixture of washing up liquid, oil, and water. This isn't really

Here are a couple of easy ways to provide insect homes (bug boxes) even on a small balcony:

1. Bundle up some twigs or bamboo canes (cut them short to keep them manageable) and tie them up with string, then hang them up under a railing. I've done this on my balcony.

2. Cut off the bottom of a plastic drink bottle, make holes in the sides, and fill with dead leaves. Leave it somewhere damp and shady.

3. Fill a small plant pot with leaves, turn upside down, and put it somewhere damp and shady.

A bug box on the underside of my balcony rail.

a long-term solution, though, unless you want to spend a lot of time spraying your plants. Plus, your rocket will taste of washing up liquid.

Slugs and snails

One of the great advantages of growing plants in pots is that it makes it much easier to deal with slugs and snails. Simply put copper tape around the rim of each pot, and the arthropods won't bother your plants. However, be warned that they can be quite persistent – a friend found a snail that had climbed up a neighbouring wall so as to drop into her copper tape protected plant pot from above!

Copper tape is also quite expensive. If you're growing on a balcony, you may not need to bother at all – I've never seen a snail or a slug on my first floor balcony. However, this may depend on what the surrounding area is like (there is no snail or slug habitat underneath my balcony from which they might climb up).

A lower-tech option is to install slug traps, usually containing beer (sometimes known as a 'slug pub'). The downside to this is that you need to get rid of the bodies of drowned slugs afterwards. They also work better if embedded in the ground, which obviously doesn't work in a paved area. However, there is an alternative model of slug trap which uses a plastic bottle and which works even on a hard surface. Cut off the top third of the bottle, invert it, and insert it into the bottom section, so it funnels down into the rest of the bottle. Part fill it with fresh beer, and the slugs can climb up the outside to get in, but won't get out again. (A similar idea works if you're having problems with wasps, using a water and sugar solution with a smidge of washing up liquid.)

Slug nematodes are also available – these are little parasites that you water onto the soil, which the slugs ingest and then slowly die from. They can be ordered online from various garden sites, and are certified organic. In my experience they do work, but you need to keep applying them fairly regularly, and they're probably overkill for a container garden.

Caterpillars

I regularly find that in mid/late summer, my green leaves acquire a huge number of caterpillars, which can destroy a window box of rocket or lettuce in very short order. Unfortunately, the only way I've found to get rid of them is to look for them, pick them off, and throw them somewhere else (a nearby municipal flowerbed, usually). Different species of caterpillar will go for different leaves, so growing a variety may help to reduce the carnage.

I've also seen a neem oil spray suggested to discourage them (though haven't yet tried this), or a spray of cayenne pepper, water, and a tiny bit of soap to bind it. Obviously, if using this you'll need to make sure that you wash your greens before eating them yourself.

Birds

Birds can be a major hazard to your crop, especially if you have fruit; and they may try to eat seed if you don't bury it well when sowing. CDs or other shiny or noisy dangly things hung from above may scare them off; or you can net your plants, or even the entire space if it's small enough. Again, this is less likely to be a problem on an urban balcony (my local birds seem to prefer to stick to the park).

Ants

Ants can be a huge nuisance, particularly if coupled with aphids. Unfortunately, getting rid of ants is extremely difficult, especially if you want to do it in an organic way.

If you can track the nest down, repeatedly disrupting it may cause the ants to pack up home and move elsewhere. Flooding the pot where you think they've set up home may cause them to clear out; make sure as well that there's nowhere else in your space that is hospitable for them. Or you can take the plant out of the pot and shake the nest out (somewhere far away from your own space).

The old fashioned solution of pouring boiling water over the nest is also an option, although it's cruel, it's not clear how well this actually works, and it certainly won't do your plants any good if you pour boiling water over their roots. Using boiling water to disrupt scent trails can be helpful, though; just pour the water over, let it dry, and repeat a couple of times. With luck, again, the ants will pack up and find somewhere else to live where their roads aren't regularly destroyed.

You could try flour sprinkled around the base of the pots to put them off (it clogs up their exoskeleton and prevents them from taking oxygen in), but it will of course wash away and/or make a terrible mess when it rains. A little cinnamon sprinkled around where you've seen ants also apparently works well, as it will disrupt their scent trails, and again, will tend to cause them to pack up and leave. I tried this together with flooding them out when I got ants on my balcony, and found that it worked temporarily, but that I had to reapply the cinnamon several times.

If remotely possible, the best and easiest option is to learn to tolerate the ants – live and let live. Having said that, if (as with my local ants) they invade your wormery and kill all the worms, you may feel more like declaring war. If I ever win, I'll let you know...

Guerilla Gardening with Unwanted Seeds

It's usually around this time of year that you discover that you have a handful of spare seedlings, or half a packet of spare seeds. (Some seeds will keep until the next year, but not all of them – carrots are a notable case of seeds which simply won't keep, so you may as well either sow or find homes for all of your seeds.)

You can just throw them away, but I always find that wasteful (and sad, in the case of the seedlings). Friends may be interested in doing seed swaps (as discussed on p.56), or you may be able to palm off seedlings on them to encourage them to start doing a little gardening themselves – feel free to chuck in a copy of this book! Local garden or allotment clubs may also organise seed or plant swaps (try an online search for local garden clubs in your area).

Alternatively, you can do your bit to brighten up your local area, and do a little guerrilla gardening. There's more information on this on p.118, but the basics are: keep an eye out for neglected patches of earth around your local area, then get out there and send your unwanted seeds and seedlings out into the world.

Summer and Winter Savory

Summer and winter savory are related varieties of the 'savories' group of around 30 species. Winter savory is hardier and is an evergreen perennial (so you should be able to harvest it all year round), while summer savory is an annual. Both have a spicy, peppery flavour, but summer savory is a bit lighter in taste.

Growing

Both types of savory like a lot of sun. Winter savory will do better in a light soil, while summer savory prefers richer soil.

Summer savory is best started off indoors; sow the seeds about 3mm deep, and it should take around three weeks for them to germinate. Alternatively, direct sow outside after the last frost, but bear in mind that you need to keep the seeds moist for them to germinate, so it may be easier to sow them inside. Plant out after about seven weeks.

Winter savory is started in much the same way, but is as easy to sow and grow outside as inside; so you can save yourself a certain among of trouble and sow directly in the pot which will be the plant's final location.

You can start to harvest after about six weeks, and then harvest normally after another month. Leaves can be dried: cut the branches off (before flowering), and hang them upside down in a warm, well-ventilated place. Remove the leaves from the branches before storing them.

Culinary uses

Savory is the traditional flavouring for bean and lentil soups. Tomatoes and savory also get on well, so try it in any of your tomato dishes. Winter savory, being a bit stronger, goes well with strong meat dishes and hearty bean-based stews. Summer savory can go well with fish, eggs, and cheese, as well as vegetable dishes, and tastes good with mixes of other herbs.

Medicinal uses

Savory tea or infusion can help with stomach upsets and mild sore throats, and a sprig of savory applied to a wasp sting is said to alleviate the pain. Savory also has a reputation for affecting sex drive – winter savory is said to reduce it and summer savory to increase it!

CHAPTER 8

JUNE

June and July are mostly about doing a lot of watering, and harvesting and eating things. You'll also need to do some thinning and pinching-out of various plants in June, to encourage them to grow better. Rocket and lettuce are also very prone to bolting right now, so you might be a bit short of salad leaves until the weather cools a little.

. . . .

My Balcony at the Start of June

Plants growing:

Herbs: sage, mint, rosemary, bay, thyme, chives, oregano, basil, parsley.

Early **dwarf peas** now over and taken out; **mangetout** doing well.

Bronze arrowhead lettuce.

Rocket and **ruby chard** gone to seed; waiting for seed to mature to harvest it.

Mispoona nearly ready to be harvested.

Tomato plants outside in pots and starting to flower.

One very small **pepper** seedling recently moved outside.

Pot of **carrots**: first edible thinnings ready.

Box of **potatoes**.

Satsuma tree starting to bloom.

Seeds and cuttings:

Second pot **carrots** still not appeared.

Dill seedlings growing well.

Papalo seedling growing well.

One **nasturtium** has come up; no marigolds.

Courgette seedlings hardening off outside.

Miscellaneous Other:

- Alarming lack of worms – possibly attacked by ants?

. . . .

Things to Do in June

- Plant out courgettes into full size pots (p.111).

- Plant out any remaining tomato or pepper seedlings (if you started any late) (p.106).

- Succession sowing of some lettuce (not rocket, which bolts very quickly if sown in June).

- Sow microgreens (p.128).

- Pinch out tomato side shoots (p.109).

- Fertilise regularly (p.119 for fertiliser).

Midsummer Problems

June weather can be a bit unpredictable in the UK, but the days are nevertheless visibly lengthening towards midsummer, and a lot of plants react to this by bolting (going to seed). Rocket is particularly notorious for this; don't even bother to sow rocket in June as it'll bolt as soon as it is big enough to eat. (The exception to this rule is if you're growing it as a microgreen and harvesting it as soon as it has a couple of real leaves.)

If you do see green leafy plants starting to bolt (they'll get suddenly much taller and start growing flower heads), you can get a bit more time out of them by pinching off the flower heads. This is very much a short-term solution, though, as they'll just grow more heads. You may be better off letting them bolt, and saving seeds for any plants that will breed true. Rocket, coriander, and parsley are all worth saving seeds from. In the case of plants such as coriander, dill and fennel, the seeds themselves are also a nice crop.

Of course, some plants you actively want to encourage to flower – any fruiting plants need to flower before they can set fruit. This includes peas, beans, tomatoes and peppers (although early peas and beans will already have started to flower, and later ones are unlikely to do so until a little later in the season). Getting your tomatoes out and growing by the start of June will encourage them to get on with flowering, after which you'll start seeing small tomatoes. You can also start using a potassium-heavy fertiliser such as comfrey tea (see p.121) to encourage flowering. See p.109 for a discussion of pinching out tomato side shoots when the plants start to set fruit.

It's also important to be aware, now it's definitely summer, that if the weather is good, your plants will get thirsty fast.

The importance of water

For tomatoes, peppers, and other water-greedy plants, you may need to water daily over summer when it's hot (especially if you have a south-facing balcony). Make a point of going out into your space daily (this is one of the reasons why you should consider, when planning, how enjoyable it will be to spend time in your space) to keep an eye on what's going on, and to make sure that your plants aren't suffering. Plants which seem to keep getting thirsty and wilting very fast may need a bigger pot – sage is usually tolerant of dry conditions, but I had to repot my sage seedling sooner than I'd expected as it was suffering from thirst. For the majority of plants, you should water before the plant starts showing signs of thirst, as that puts it under unwanted stress and may affect its production. Keep an eye instead on the soil moisture and water when that becomes too dry (although be aware that 'too dry' varies between plants). Self-watering containers (see p.73) will also help here, especially for tomatoes and other thirsty plants.

If the space allows it, a water butt with drainpipe diverter will help.

If tomatoes don't get enough water, you may get blossom end rot (a large brown or black area on the bottom of the tomato). This is most likely to happen at the start of the season if a sudden hot spell hits and there isn't enough water for the plants. If you see this, pull the affected fruit off and throw away. Blossom end rot can also be caused by too much water, so the soil should be damp but not soaking. Too much water, or irregular watering, can also cause the fruit to crack, although in this case you can still eat them, as cracking only affects the look, not the taste, of the fruit. Ideally, water well in the evening (if it's really hot, in the morning as well); or use self-watering containers for the best results. It's best not to water in the heat of the day as the water will evaporate faster, thus wasting some of your effort. You should also do your best to avoid getting water on the leaves of the plants if watering in the morning, as this can lead to the sun scorching the leaves.

If you don't water potatoes enough, especially in the early stages when they're setting their tubers, you'll get fewer and smaller potatoes when you come to harvest them. Potatoes are best served by heavy weekly waterings rather than by little-and-often watering. See p.24 for more on plants, water and water sources.

Thinning plants

Plants, once they've germinated, need a certain amount of room to grow, and you may find yourself needing to thin your seedlings out a bit.

Self-seeded basil seedlings growing underneath a bigger plant which I overwintered.

When thinning, think about how big you expect the leaves of your plants to get. If therer isn't enough room between plants to spread their leaves out, they'll grow tall, thin, and straggly, as they try to get enough light. They also need room for their roots to grow. Plants that are too close together will steal nutrition from each other. In practice, what tends to happen is that one plant in each group will start to do better, and the others will be stunted; but the strong plant could be even stronger if it weren't competing with the others for sun, water, and nutrients.

Having said that, it is entirely possible to grow plants at a closer spacing than is suggested on the packet. As with many of these things, the best bet is to experiment a bit and see how your plants do.

With some plants (e.g. carrots, rocket, and other salad leaves) you can eat the thinnings, which is nice as it increases your crop yield. With others, you'll just have to stick the thinnings in the compost.

There are two basic approaches to thinning:

1. Sow to the desired density in the first place. This way, you won't have to thin at all, so it saves effort; but if not all of your seeds germinate, you'll have fewer plants than you wanted. It's almost always a good idea to sow a couple of extra seeds. In my experience, the larger the seeds, the higher the germination rate – so sow more rocket seeds than you would courgette seeds.

2. Sow more than you want to end up with, and thin as the plants come up. This is more effort (although you still get some benefit if you can eat the thinnings) but your chances of getting the number of plants you want is higher.

Of course, you can also take a middle road; and as you get more knowledgeable about the plants you're growing, you will have a better idea of the germination rate you can expect. I've tried to indicate which plants have particularly bad germination rates (e.g. carrots) or good rates (e.g. courgettes).

If you've sown very thickly, you'll probably need to do a little thinning as soon as the seedlings come up. Take a pair of scissors, and carefully snip out the weakest seedlings from each group. Using scissors avoids upsetting the roots of the stronger seedling (the one you want to keep), which might affect its growth. With very tiny seedlings you can use a sharp fingernail.

For plants whose thinnings you can't eat, you can thin straight to the desired spacing as soon as they've germinated (although you may want to leave a couple of extras in case something happens to the stronger seedlings). For plants where you want to eat the thinnings, thin to maybe half or even a third of the desired spacing on the first round, then leave them for a couple of weeks and thin again. With carrots in particular, the longer you can get away with leaving it the better; but if you wait too long, the plants that remain will not grow as large as they might.

This rocket may be slower to go to seed if you thin it a bit as it grows.

These lettuces are doing well so far but could definitely use thinning before they get any bigger. The thinnings will make a substantial salad!

Basil

Basil is a very well-known culinary herb which will grow vigorously in pots in a well-lit area over the summer. It's not cold-hardy, but you may be able to keep it alive over the winter if you can bring it in to a sunny windowsill. It's technically a 'tender perennial', which means that you can keep it alive for years if it's kept warm all year round, but most people treat it as an annual. If you are trying to keep a plant growing for more than a year, make sure you save seed when it flowers in case it either gets too knobbly to be great for leaves, or gets too cold and dies. I've kept a basil plant going for 18 months, but never managed longer than that.

In theory it will grow all year round inside, whilst in my experience it doesn't do much growing over winter proper. You'll get a head start when you take it outdoors again, but don't do this before the last frost! You'll probably want to sow a few more plants as well.

There are several varieties of basil, but if you're only growing one, it's probably sweet basil that you want. There are a couple of 'true' perennial basils, African Blue basil and Thai basil, so if you're keen on perennial plants (a very permaculture-oriented decision!) you can try those out. They can also be propagated from cuttings. Note that these don't have the same taste as sweet basil, although Thai basil is frequently used in Asian cooking.

Growing

Basil really doesn't like frost, so if sowing outside, it's vital to wait until after your last frost date. Alternatively, you can sow inside a bit earlier, and move outside after the last frost has passed.

Sow seeds fairly thinly, and cover them with 5mm of compost. Once the seedlings have developed two pairs of true leaves, thin to leave only the strongest seedlings. The true leaves are the ones that come in after the very first seedling leaves that you see when the plant first appears above the soil.

If you're a fan of basil, you'll know that you can use quite a lot of it in cooking, so sow as many seedlings as you have the space for! You can fit several plants in a 23cm pot. Regular potting compost is fine as a growing material. Add a little fertiliser (see p.119) every month or so.

Pinch the tops out regularly (and eat the leaves!) to discourage running to seed and to promote bushiness. If your basil does run to seed, save the seeds and resow. It will keep producing leaves afterwards, although some people find that some varieties change taste after they go to seed. You can resow more or less any time during the summer, although the later it is in the season, the less use you'll get out of the plants before you have to either take them in or sacrifice them to the first frosts.

Culinary uses

Basil is most often useful in tomato-based pasta sauces (it goes well with oregano). You can also use it to make pesto, or add it to salads.

To make pesto, put 1.5 cups of fresh basil leaves, 1 cup Parmesan cheese, 1 cup pine nuts, 1/3 cup olive oil, salt and pepper to taste, and 2 cloves of garlic into a blender. Blend until the texture is right. Add more garlic to taste.

To make this recipe vegan, simply leave out the Parmesan and add 1/3 cup nutritional yeast if you have any. (And note that not all Parmesan is strictly vegetarian, so some vegetarians may prefer the vegan version too.)

Medicinal uses

Basil has digestive properties when drunk as a tea, and can be used to reduce gas. It's also recommended for stomach cramps, vomiting, and constipation; and can be helpful as a remedy against anxiety.

To make basil tea, steep a few leaves in boiling water for 5-10 minutes, and drink after dinner. Some people find it acts as a slight sedative, so it may also be useful to relax you after a stressful day.

CHAPTER 7

JULY

July is all about the harvesting and eating... but it's also a good time to begin to think about what you want to grow in the autumn, and to start sowing for that. July is also the time for propagating strawberries. And hopefully for sitting out in the sunshine and enjoying spending time in your very own green edible jungle.

. . . .

My Balcony at the Start of July

Plants growing:

Around eight **tomato** plants, with the first trusses of tomatoes coming along well.

Herbs: sage, mint, rosemary, bay, thyme, chives, oregano, basil, parsley, dill, papalo, coriander.

Bronze arrowhead lettuce mostly gone to seed.

Microgreens along the edge of the railing.

Two pots of **carrots** (first baby carrots already eaten).

Two **courgette** plants beginning to flower.

Satsuma tree putting out plenty of leaves.

Box of **potatoes**.

Nasturtiums and **marigolds** starting to show up.

A late sowing of **mangetout** just beginning to appear.

Pepper seedling still growing very slowly.

Seeds and cuttings: none

*Papalo plant
doing well.*

Things to Do in July

- Keep an eye on the courgettes and fertilise them by hand if need be (p.112).

- Harvest early potatoes.

- Begin sowing hardy lettuce for autumn (p.149).

- Start sowing rocket and other greens again.

- Sow lamb's lettuce (corn salad) and land cress for winter salads.

- Harvest first tomatoes (if you're in the south and lucky with the weather).

- Pinch out tomato growing tips if necessary (p.109).

- Harvest carrots.

- Consider sowing late carrots, beets, and chard (p.101).

- Take oregano cuttings (p.102).

Strawberry Runners for Next Year

From about June or July, strawberry plants start trying to propagate themselves by sending out runners (long vines that snake along the ground). Each runner will produce little clone plants at intervals, looking for some soil to touch down and root in. Once the baby clone has rooted, the runner dies off, and you have a new strawberry plant.

If you already have strawberries on your balcony, you can watch for these runners starting to appear, at which point you have a couple of options. You can peg them down back into the original trough, but it may then get overcrowded. However, strawberry plants only last three years (you'll get a small crop in year one, a large one in year two, and maybe a large-ish crop in year three, but that's your lot), so you may be able to get the timing right so you can use the runners to replace old plants.

Alternatively, you can peg them down into another trough, or into small pots. You can then cut the runners once the clone plant has rooted firmly, and either move the new trough elsewhere, or transplant from the small pots into a permanent location. Cut off any surplus runners and discard.

Strawberry runners looking for a new home.

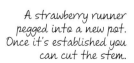

A strawberry runner pegged into a new pot. Once it's established you can cut the stem.

Don't let the runner plant crop in its very first summer (when it's just rooted itself); pinch off any flowers that appear. In the autumn, you can plant it into its final location.

If you don't have strawberry plants already, now is the time to ask around friends and neighbours for anyone who does have plants and who therefore will have runners that may be surplus to requirements. It's best not to just cut the clone plants off, but to provide your strawberry grower with a small pot or two to peg the runners down into. This way the new plants have a chance to root, and develop a little strength, before they're cut off from their parent.

If on the other hand you find yourself with an excess of baby plants yourself, you can peg them into small pots as described above, and then when the plants are established, cut the runners and give the plants away as presents. Strawberries are simple to grow, do well in window boxes, and are a great intro to food container gardening. If you've saved excess rocket seed, you can give out pinches of that, too, to sow next to the strawberries. You could also consider planting them in neglected public spaces, see p.118 for more on guerrilla gardening.

Strawberries are discussed more generally on p.114.

Thinking about Autumn

Hardy lettuces

It may seem a bit early to be thinking about autumn, but in fact it's about the right time to begin sowing hardy lettuces in order to get them going by early autumn. You can keep sowing through the rest of the summer and early autumn, but sowing some now means that you'll have mature plants as well as younger ones by the time the weather starts getting colder.

Bronze arrowhead lettuce is a good overwinter crop; rocket and mizuna also work well; and you can get other winter lettuces that are bred to tolerate the cold. Get a few plants in now, and plan to sow some more in August to make sure that you have plenty of plants at various stages, and in case a sudden spell of hot weather later on in the summer makes them bolt again. You can sow as late as September, especially if you're in the south, but you may find that the plants take a long while to get established. Helpfully, you may find that some of your earlier sowings of lettuce, rocket, and other greens have bolted by now. Collect the seeds from them when they're ready, and sow them again. See p.84 for discussion of growing green leaves.

My south-facing balcony at the height of summer.

You could also try late sowings of other vegetables. Carrots (see p.88) can be sown late (although my results with this have been variable), especially

if you only want to grow them to salad size rather than to maincrop size. Plants such as tomatoes and peppers that need to ripen won't be much good sown this late; but I have sown tomatoes on a south-facing balcony in July, and got a handful of ripe tomatoes in late September and early October, before making green tomato chutney (see p.37) with the rest of the crop. If you don't mind an unripe crop, and have some space, it may be worth a go. If you do this, you should start the plants inside to get them going as quickly as possible, and be sure to harden them off (by putting them out for a few hours a day and bringing them inside overnight) for a couple of days before putting them out permanently.

Peas can also be sown late for a late summer/early autumn crop. Peas tend not to like the really hot weather of midsummer, so you may actually find that they do better sown in July and cropping in August than they do sown in June and cropping in July. However, the vagaries of the UK's weather do make this a bit of a guess. In places with more reliably hot late summer weather, this probably isn't worth trying.

The important thing to remember here is that it's fine just to experiment. Some of those experiments will work out well, and you'll manage to get more food out of your space. Some of them won't work out, and you'll have to write them off to experience. Whatever happens, you're learning about your space, your climate (or microclimate), and about the plants, so even failures are useful information.

Fennel

Fennel is a beautiful perennial which is a pretty addition to the herb garden; it's also tasty and has medicinal properties. The yellow flowers may also attract beneficial insects. With this many uses, it's well worth growing in a small space.

There are three types of fennel: Florence fennel, which is grown for its bulb (which is eaten as a vegetable); common fennel (a wild plant, not used in cooking), and sweet fennel, which is what you're likely to want to grow and what I discuss here. Florence fennel is grown very similarly (and may even do better in a pot than sweet fennel); you can eat the foliage of Florence fennel, but you harvest the bulb before the plant goes to seed, so you can't get fennel seed from it.

Growing

Fennel likes full sun and well-drained soil. Sow seeds directly in the soil in late spring and cover with 6mm of soil, sowing in succession to get a constant supply of leaves. Fennel is a perennial but will happily reseed itself, so keep an eye out for seedlings and be prepared to pull them up if you don't want it established in *all* of your pots!

Once the seedlings are established, thin to one per 25-30cm pot. If you wait for a little while and allow the plants to grow a bit, you should be able to use the bulb of the thinnings in cooking. Note that fennel will not do well in smaller pots (mine died in a 15cm pot). Keep the soil moist but not too wet, and ideally put it in full sun, although it will tolerate partial shade. Make sure that the soil drains well.

If you allow the plant to flower, you can harvest and use the seeds once they're ripe. If you'd rather just use the foliage, you can remove the flower heads as they appear to encourage more leafy growth.

Note that if you want to harvest the seeds, you should keep fennel away from coriander or dill, as they may cross-fertilise (although there is some debate about the actual likelihood of this). This won't affect the foliage or the seeds in the current plants, but will produce seeds which won't breed true for the next year's plants. Fennel doesn't get on with tomatoes or potatoes, either, so don't grow them in the same pot. It's said in fact to be allopathic to many other plants (inhibiting growth, or in some cases killing them off), although not all gardeners notice these effects. However, to avoid potential problems it's best kept in a pot by itself. It's also very quick to self-seed so can be quite invasive if you don't keep an eye on the seedlings.

Culinary uses

Fennel bulb can be eaten raw (it has a slightly aniseed-like taste), or used in salad or Italian food; it's also very nice roasted in olive oil with other root vegetables.

Fennel leaf can be used in fish dishes (whole leaves can be used to roast fish on) or soup; it tastes slightly of liquorice. Fennel is also particularly widely used in Greek cooking, particularly in stews and fritters. It should be added just at the end of cooking to avoid losing its flavour.

Fennel seeds can be eaten as a snack or to freshen the breath after a meal (as is common in parts of Pakistan and India); or used in sauces. It's commonly used to flavour rye bread in Scandinavia, and in sausages in Italy. It's also used in some Indian cooking, as part of poran, a spice blend that also includes fenugreek and cumin seed.

Medicinal uses

Fennel tea, made with a teaspoon of crushed fennel seed, can be used as a digestive aid and system cleanser, or as a breath freshener. Chewing fennel seed is also a good breath freshener. Eating fennel can increase the flow of milk in nursing mothers, and may help ease symptoms for menopausal women. Fennel water can be used as a 'gripe water' for babies, although babies shouldn't consume too much fennel as it may cause premature breast bud development (this is known as 'thelarche' and is a benign and self-limiting condition).

Fennel has anti-flea properties, so use it in pet bedding to help if your dog or cat has a flea problem.

It also makes a good steam facial, opening the pores and cleansing the skin. Boil a tablespoon of crushed fennel seed in water for five minutes, then transfer it to a large bowl. Wash your face in warm water, then put your head over the bowl and cover it with a towel to keep the steam in, and stay there for 5-10 minutes.

AUGUST

More harvesting and eating the produce in August, and hopefully more enjoying the sunshine. You can also experiment with a late potato sowing, if you have a couple of spare seed potatoes; and you'll need to think about seed saving as various plants go to seed.

. . . .

My Balcony at the Start of August

Plants growing:

- Eight **tomato** plants, with plenty of ripening tomatoes.

- **Herbs**: sage, mint, rosemary, bay, thyme, chives, oregano, basil, parsley, dill, papalo, coriander.

- **Bronze arrowhead lettuce**: a few new plants coming up.

- **Microgreens** along the edge of the railing.

- Two pots of **carrots** (first baby carrots already eaten).

- **Courgette** plant, without as yet any courgettes.

- **Satsuma** tree putting out plenty of leaves, but no sign of fruit.

- **Nasturtiums** and **marigolds** scattered in various pots (see p.116 for more on companion planting).

- Late sowing of **mangetout** doing well.

- **Pepper** plant without flowers or peppers yet.

Seeds and cuttings: none.

Things to Do in August

- Keep an eye on the courgettes and fertilise them by hand if need be (p.112).
- Harvest potatoes.
- Harvest tomatoes, carrots, and courgettes as they fruit.
- Succession sowing of rockets and other greens.
- Potential late sowing of potatoes (p.161).
- Other experimental late sowings (p.151).
- Seed saving as plants run to seed (p.158).
- Preserving any glut of produce (p.156).

Harvesting and Preserving

Growing things is great, but if you're lucky, you may also face the question of what to do with them. In most cases, in a small space, you'll to be able to keep up with eating what you produce as you produce it, most of the time. However, some vegetables tend to show up all at once (tomatoes may do this, depending on which varieties you chose and how many plants you grow), and you can also end up with a lot of green veg which are about to go to seed all at once, and so instead you prefer to harvest them all at once. The solution to this is preserving, which can take various forms.

Freezing

The most straightforward way to preserve food is to freeze it, which is particularly good for soft fruit. Raspberries, strawberries, blackcurrants, and blueberries all freeze well, and getting out a spoonful of frozen home-grown strawberries for your morning muesli in December is both satisfying and cheering. Dry the fruit as much as possible before freezing it, to avoid freezer burn.

To get individual frozen fruit rather than a huge lump of frozen fruit, you need to flash freeze the fruit. Get a baking sheet, or a sheet of tinfoil, and lay the fruit out in a single layer on it, not touching. Put it flat in the freezer for 24 hours. Once the fruit have frozen, take them off the baking sheet and put them into a labelled box – they'll now stay separate and you can eat however much you want at a time!

Frozen fruit are nice in smoothies, porridge, muesli or yoghurt, or just on their own. You can also use them to bake with (try crumble or stew).

Blanching

A good option for green veg such as chard or spinach is blanching, followed by freezing. Blanching destroys various enzymes and bacteria, helping to keep the food fresh, and also maintains its colour and texture.

Use a pan with a lid, so that you can get the temperature back up to boiling as fast as possible. Fill the pan with water and bring it to the boil, and put your clean produce to be blanched into a sieve or chip basket (this is just to keep it all together). Once the water is boiling, plunge the sieve into the water, and put the lid back on the pan – the water needs to be back to boiling in under a minute. If necessary, you can blanch smaller quantities at a time. Courgettes (sliced) should be blanched for a minute, chard or spinach for two minutes.

Once the time is up, remove the sieve and plunge into a bowl of cold water for a few seconds, then into a bowl of water with icecubes in. This stops the cooking process (if the veg are left to cool by themselves, they'll carry on cooking in their own heat). Once it's cooled, dry and put into the freezer. See above for how to flash freeze if you want to keep the veg separate; otherwise, just freeze in appropriate portion sizes.

Bottling/canning tomatoes

Finally, with tomatoes and some other vegetables, you can try bottling (also known as canning). The downside of this is that you'll need to invest in a certain amount of kit – at the very least, sufficient jars and lids to hold your crop, and a pan large enough to boil the jars in (this seals them). Reusable lids are available and are worthwhile in the long run, but do cost more in the short term. You can either bottle your tomatoes whole (blanch them first, for one minute) or turn them into sauce first. Making sauce has the advantage that it shrinks the tomatoes down a bit and therefore you need fewer jars. If you decide to try bottling (I have never quite had enough tomatoes yet to be worth it!), there's plenty of further information available online. Be aware that since bottling doesn't use sugar or vinegar to help with the preservation, you need to be more careful about sterilisation of your equipment and making certain that the jars come up to temperature. Jam or chutney is more forgiving as the sugar content makes it harder for any nasties to survive.

You can also turn green tomatoes into green tomato chutney (see p.37) or just leave them in the fridge to ripen slowly.

Jams and jellies

Another option for preserving fruit is to make jam or jelly. The basic approach is to use the same weight in sugar as fruit, put it all into a heavy-bottomed saucepan, and leave on a low heat, stirring often, while it first melts and then thickens. Meanwhile, wash some jars and put them (but not their lids) into the oven at 100°C to sterilise.

When making jam, you use the whole fruit and leave it in; jelly is made in much the same way but with the fruit juice only. There's a recipe for hawthorn and rosehip jelly on p.171. Chutney is also a form of savoury jam, again made in much the same way; see p.37 for a recipe for green tomato chutney.

If making other jams, you should remember that some fruit needs added pectin (blackberries, raspberries and other berries) in order to set, whereas others (such as rhubarb and apple) have their own pectin. If you're adding pectin, you should only need to cook the jam after the sugar has melted for a short while. Follow the instructions on the pectin packet for best results. You can also chop up an apple (whole, including skin and core) and suspend it in the jam in a muslin bag to make your own pectin. However, I've had limited success with this. I did come out with some very nice rosehip syrup-ish stuff; it just didn't really set.

If you're making jam without added pectin, you need to boil it for longer, and test it intermittently for setting. Put a saucer in the fridge to get cold, then drop a teaspoon of jam onto the saucer and leave it to cool for a moment. If when you drag a finger across it, it has formed a skin, it has set, and you should take the jam off the boil and pour it into the sterilised jars. (I strongly recommend using a funnel to avoid making a terrible mess.) Place a circle of greaseproof paper on top (you can buy packets of circles specifically for jam making) and put the lid on. Label the jars with contents and date once cool.

Saving Seed as Plants Run to Seed or Die Off

As mentioned on p.57, the big advantage of growing your plants from 'real' seeds (i.e. seeds that have been open pollinated and which will breed true) rather than from the F1 hybrids you'll get in garden centres is that it enables you, if you wish, to save seeds from the plants that you grow.

Seed saving is definitely optional, especially if you're a beginner gardener. If you're not interested or don't fancy it, it's fine to stick with buying seeds from a shop. But if you do want to try out seed saving, it does mean that you can both save money by buying fewer seeds next year, and that you can select seeds from plants that grew particularly well in your space, or that tasted particularly good. Effectively you're selecting for success: so next year's plants from those saved seeds should also do slightly better, and then you can again save seed from the best of that crop. Over a period of years, you can select for any characteristics you like: early (or late) cropping, particularly sweet tomatoes, resistance to bolting... it's up to you!

Bear in mind that not all plants are easy to save seed from. Tomatoes are easy, as they always self-fertilise so will always breed true. Rocket, parsley, chives, and dill are also easy to save the seeds of. In other cases, such as chard, the plants are wind-pollinated, so may be inclined to cross with plants from elsewhere. This means that it's nearly impossible to be sure what you'll get in the next generation. The seeds should grow *something*, though, so feel free to experiment if you want! I've made a note in the discussion of each plant whether seed saving is or is not possible.

It's important to find a way to keep track of which plants have been particularly successful. If you're selecting for the tastiest tomato, for example, it's too late to decide to save seeds when most of the tomatoes have gone, because you may not be able to identify the best taste any more. If you're selecting for quantity produced, then you'll need to label each plant right at the start, and then track the weight (this is more useful than number) of fruit obtained from each plant. (This is, admittedly, a bit of a hassle for the home gardener.) If you're selecting for resistance to bolting, the easiest way to do this is to watch for the first handful of plants to bolt, then tag all of the ones that have not yet done so. As each

Bruschetta with Salad

Cherry tomatoes can pretty much be eaten as is, and they go very well with a random assortment of microgreens or full sized leaves, especially rocket.

Another option is to slice them into quarters and make bruschetta. Mix the chopped tomatoes with some chopped garlic, olive oil, and vinegar, and set aside. Toast the bread, then rub a clove of garlic on one side, and drizzle a little olive oil on. Top with the tomato mixture and some basil leaves, and serve with green leafy salad on the side.

plant bolts, take its tag off: the last tag to stay on identifies the plant you want. Otherwise, by the time they've all bolted, you won't be able to tell which one was which.

Remember with all of these characteristics that other factors will also affect the outcome. Were all the pots the same size and made of the same material? Did you water all of the plants evenly (and were any of them in self-watering containers)? Did you feed them all evenly? Were some in more shade than others? My most successful tomato plant the year I wrote this book was in the sunniest spot on the balcony, against a brick wall, in a self-watering container. I am pretty sure that its success was more down to these factors than to genetics; although I saved some seed anyway, and will certainly grow another plant or two in that spot next year!

For fruiting plants, you also need to remember that you want to save some seeds before you eat all of the fruit. Save seed from a healthy, successful-looking fruit, not from a small weedy one. Saving seed from green leafy plants is easier, because you won't be eating them after they've bolted; although bear in mind that you may want to make sure you do leave one or two plants to bolt after you've eaten the rest, so don't crop the whole lot.

With green leafy plants, keep an eye on the plants after they've flowered, until you see the seed cases developing and starting to dry out. It's best to leave them on the plant for as long as possible, but do take them off and finish the drying process on the windowsill before they're entirely done, or they'll self-seed all over your pots instead. Parsley and rocket are both particular culprits for this, in my experience; happily I very much like both plants so am not too bothered by their ubiquitous vigour! If they spread too much, I just eat more of them. Alternatively, if you prefer a more *laissez faire* approach, just let them self-seed and don't bother saving any. I prefer to do both, so I have some seed for the next year if the self-seeding was insufficient or in awkward places.

Bronze arrowhead lettuce seedheads.

With fruiting plants such

Seed inside a rocket seedpod.

as tomatoes, just cut the seeds out and spread them on a plate to dry (don't use kitchen towel, or they'll stick). Alternatively, you can put the tomatoes in water for a bit to ferment, which will help to separate out the seeds, and also help them to germinate faster next year. Just scoop the seeds out and put them in a jar with some water, stir, and leave for a few days. Cover the jar with a piece of kitchen roll, held on with an elastic band, to minimise fruit fly problems. The fermentation is finished when there's a layer of mould on the top, and/or the seeds have all settled to the bottom of the mixture. Strain the seeds into a sieve, and rinse well. Drain them and spread them on a plate to dry.

Once your seeds, of whatever type, have fully dried, you can extract them carefully from their seed cases or pick them off the plate, and put them into a sealable packet of some kind (both paper and plastic are fine). Label the packets with plant, date, and location, and put them somewhere cool, dry, and dark until spring.

Sowing Potatoes for Christmas Dinner

By now, your earlier-planted potatoes should have been dug up and eaten; and hopefully they were tasty! It's not too late now to sow a very early (or possibly very late) batch of seed potatoes to come up for Christmas dinner, or at least for sometime in the late autumn or early winter. Remember that potatoes take about 16 weeks to be ready to pull up (and will grow a little more slowly in the late summer/autumn), so depending on the variety you have and when you'd like to eat them, you can either go ahead and sow them now, or wait until early September. Given that the days are getting shorter at this time of year, you're better off sowing a bit early and leaving them in the ground once they're grown, than sowing them bang on time, as the plants are likely to take a bit longer to get growing at this time of year. See p.97 for more on growing potatoes in containers.

While writing this book I tried a second sowing of potatoes once I'd dug up the first ones (and dealt with the ants' nest that I found in the bottom of the box). I sowed them just as discussed on p.97. They grew normally, and I earthed them up as they got bigger, and watered regularly. I eventually dug the potatoes up the following New Year. I got only a bare handful of smallish potatoes, but it was enough for a meal for me and they were very tasty! The seed potatoes would otherwise have been thrown away, so it was worth the (minimal) effort. It wouldn't have been worth acquiring seed potatoes specifically for this, however, unless you're very enthusiastic about the idea.

HERB OF THE MONTH

Mint

Mint is notoriously easy to grow and hard to kill – though I confess I have managed it. It does particularly well in pots since it's so determined to self-perpetuate that even in gardens or allotments it's recommended that you put it in a pot and sink the pot in the ground, to stop it taking the whole place over. It can also tolerate shady conditions, but it does require regular watering.

Growing

I grew my mint from a cutting that was perhaps a little closer to a root division. Mint propagates underground, so if you take a sprig from an established plant and get even a fairly small piece of root with it, then stick it in a pot of compost, it'll probably settle in just fine. Always take two or three cuttings in case one doesn't take. Be warned that it may take a while to get started; be patient. If it hasn't actually withered and gone brown, it's probably fine. (Later, with established mint, even if it does wither and die off, there's probably enough life in the roots that it can be resurrected with a little TLC.)

You can also grow mint easily from seed – just sow the seed and keep the soil moist.

Mint likes moist conditions, and will tolerate shade well. If in full sun, remember to water it regularly. A larger pot may help it retain more water. Given half a chance it will spread, but in a container you should be fine! Feed monthly with a liquid fertiliser of some sort.

Mint cutting doing well – notice the little leaves sprouting from the base of the larger ones. The label refers to the fact that I got the cutting from my friend Jess.

Culinary uses

One of the nicest uses for mint is in making mint tea – simply pour boiling water over a sprig of mint, or for a stronger flavour, simmer the mint briefly in water on the stove. Mint is also nice in cocktails, try vodka, apple juice and a sprig of mint.)

New potatoes and fresh peas are nice with a few leaves of mint, and you can of course make mint sauce. Mint is also used in Moroccan cooking.

Medicinal uses

Mint tea is good for settling the stomach, whether the trouble is indigestion, trapped wind or nausea, and can be pleasantly rehydrating. It's also recommended to treat menstrual cramps. It is said to be useful for kidney or liver problems, although there's no evidence of this.

A mint poultice can be used to treat headache or backache (use a compress soaked in a mint decoction, where the mint has been boiled in the water for a few minutes).

SEPTEMBER

By September, the main growing season is starting to be over, although hopefully you've planned ahead to get your autumn veg in. You can still sow some more now, though, to keep you going through the winter. It's also a good time for foraging for berries (as is October, and rosehips will be good through to November).

· ·

My Balcony at the Start of September

Plants growing:

Eight **tomato** plants, still with plenty of ripening tomatoes.

Herbs: sage, mint, rosemary, bay, thyme, chives, oregano, basil, parsley, dill, papalo, coriander.

New self-seeded **bronze arrowhead lettuce** doing well.

Rocket and **mizuna** along the edge of the railing.

Two pots of **carrots** with a couple of carrots left.

Courgette plant on its last legs (it never did well this year, unfortunately).

Satsuma tree still alive but no actual satsumas.

Nasturtiums and **marigolds** in various pots.

Pepper plant showing a single flower.

· ·

Things to Do in September

- **Harvest** tomatoes.
- **Sow** salad leaves for autumn and winter.
- **Sow** autumn greens (p.165).
- **Foraging** for wild berries (p.169).

Bringing Delicate Herbs Inside for the Winter

In my experience, September weather can be a little unpredictable; sometimes it's glorious sunshine right until the end, sometimes the autumn has clearly set in by the middle of the month. The details of this will depend on your local climate. Further north, it may be reliably moving into autumn by mid-September. However, it's not unusual to get patches of sunny weather quite late in September, so for moderately cold-hardy plants, there's no need to rush them into shelter until it definitely is becoming cold. Keep an eye on the weather forecast!

However, by the end of September you will want to bring in herbs that aren't hardy enough to overwinter; basil is one obvious candidate. Basil kept indoors will sometimes survive the winter; see p.44 for more.

Some other herbs such as rosemary and sage will do fine over the winter without any protection; some, such as oregano and thyme, will survive but will only carry on producing at all if you protect them in a cold frame (see p.38) or mini-greenhouse. There are also other options for protecting larger delicate plants, see p.44 for more detail on wrapping up plants for the winter.

Some herbs, such as basil, won't survive at all and you'll just need to resow next spring. If you've been able to save any seed, this will be easy! Some plants (such as parsley) will probably also have self-seeded, possibly excessively so. Having said that, the year I was writing this book, we had an abnormally warm autumn in London, and I had basil seedlings outside which survived fine without a cold frame until the end of October. Be prepared to be flexible, but to be safe, you should plan to deal with the more tender plants by the end of September. Leaving it longer than that means keeping a close eye on the weather and on the forecast. Tender plants probably won't survive an early frost, unless your space is very well-protected.

For more on protecting delicate plants over the winter, see p.44.

Autumn Greens

As the days get shorter and a little chillier, it's time to plan what you want to grow over the autumn and winter. If you have a cold frame or want to make one (see p.36), you'll have a bit more scope, but there are also greens (both salad and cooked greens) that are hardy enough to survive without protection.

I've mentioned succession sowing a few times already in this book; it's a great way of making the most of a small space. Succession sowing basically means that instead of sowing all your plants at once, you spread the sowing over a few weeks, so that the plants mature at different times.

This can be particularly useful in the winter, if you want to start your seeds off on a windowsill before putting them out into the cold frame. Most greens will be ready to move out after about a fortnight; which is a useful interval for succession sowing. So move the seedlings into their larger pots, and reuse the seed tray for the next batch of seeds.

Do bear in mind that for most salad leaves, you can probably only keep sowing until late October (or very early November if you're lucky in the south, and don't mind very slow growth). Succession sowing gives you a better chance of getting older, hardier plants well-established by this stage (so they should keep growing leaves through the winter), while still giving you young, tender leaves from the later sowings for longer.

To extend the sowing season even longer, you can carry on sowing on the windowsill and keep the plants there – either in large enough pots that they'll mature properly, or as microgreens (see p.128). In the depths of winter, however, even inside they may not do too well as there's just not enough light or warmth.

Salad Greens

There are several hardy lettuces and other greens that will grow over the winter, such as bronze arrowhead lettuce and other winter lettuce, rocket, land cress, and mizuna for salads. See p.84 for more information on growing greens generally. If you're sowing in September, you should be able to get most seeds to germinate outside, particularly if it's a sunny September. However, if you want to give them a bit of a head start (often worthwhile at this time of year), you can start seeds off on a sunny windowsill, then

Mizuna

plant them on outside. If you do this, make sure to harden them off before putting them outside permanently (see p.83). It's more important to do this hardening-off when sowing in autumn than it is when sowing in the spring; the fact that it's getting colder rather than warmer means that it'll be harder (or even impossible) for the plants to make up any ground lost by the shock of a sudden temperature change when they go outside. To make the most of your autumn salad greens, take a little more care with them and introduce them gently to the outside world.

I've grown bronze arrowhead lettuce right through winter (even with snow falling), but it'll do slightly better and be more likely to keep actively producing leaves, rather than just surviving, in a cold frame. Other winter lettuce (winter lettuces are bred to cope well with low light and low temperatures) will act similarly. You could also try placing your lettuce or rocket inside the house on a sunny windowsill, if it seems to be struggling. If you have the space, experiment with plants in different situations and see which do best.

Other windowsill options include microgreens (see p.128). You can keep growing microgreens on a windowsill straight through the winter, by succession sowing in a plastic tray. You can also sprout beans and lentils throughout the winter.

Cooked greens

As well as salad greens, there are cooked greens which can be sown in autumn and grown through the winter. You can sow these seeds on the windowsill now with the intention of hardening them off and then planting them out into the pots freed up when you take your tomato plants out in October, to use your space, containers, and potting mix as efficiently as possible. Remember to feed well and if possible to add a little more of your own compost or a commercial one to the potting mix before reusing. See p.80 for more on revitalising compost and potting mix.

Kale

Kale can be grown in a pot to produce baby leaves, and is extremely hardy. Baby kale leaves can be used in salads, but they're nicer flash fried (possibly with a little garlic and ginger) or steamed (kale does a better job of reducing cholesterol when steamed). Kale is an excellent source of vitamin A and C, and a good source of iron and manganese.

Sow in early September directly where you want it to grow, cover the seeds with about 12mm of soil, and keep the soil moist until the seeds germinate. In fact, kale prefers moist soil throughout its growth period to keep its leaves sweet. Seeds will germinate a little faster indoors, so if you're sowing later in September you can start them inside and then move them out (be sure to harden them off before you put them outside permanently). Be careful not to disturb the roots too much if you're transplanting the seedlings to a larger pot after they've been hardened off.

Each plant should be in a 23-30cm pot. You should be able to start harvesting in about two months; take the outer leaves, and leave the inner ones so that the plant will keep producing. Frost is good for kale as it makes it a little sweeter!

Mustard greens

Mustard greens are very cold-hardy and will keep growing even in very bad weather. They have a very strong flavour, so use with caution, but they're nice in stir fry. You can get hotter and more mild versions, so grow according to your taste.

Sow seeds about 8mm deep, either directly to the pot you want them to end up in, or indoors if you want to speed germination up a little. Transplant (after hardening off) if necessary when they have a couple of full sets of leaves. You can get a couple of seedlings in a 30cm pot, or one per 15-20cm pot. They're a good candidate for succession sowing to keep the supply going.

Mustard greens prefer full sun but cool weather. They need plenty of water and regular feeding to keep supply up. You should be able to start harvesting in around 45 days; as with kale, pick leaves rather than the whole plant and leave the rest to keep producing. The leaves are at their nicest when young and tender.

Spinach and chard

Winter spinach is cold-hardy, and another good winter vegetable. Sow seeds in early September, around an inch deep; it's best just to sow direct. Water in well, and make sure that the soil remains moist while the seeds germinate.

Thin after around 6 weeks if necessary, then as the plant gets big enough to harvest, you can begin to pick leaves. The plant will keep growing through winter. In colder areas it may however need a cloche or a cold frame.

Chard can be treated in much the same way as spinach; you may also find that any chard you sowed earlier in the season is still going strong. There's more information on growing spinach on p.92.

Broccoli raab

Broccoli raab (which produces sprouts like sprouting broccoli, but can be harvested within 40 days) can be sown in late summer / early autumn. It's another vegetable which is nice in stir fry. I have found that broccoli raab doesn't produce much in the way of heads, but as there's not much else growing at this time of year, if you like the taste, it's worth growing, especially as you end up with spare pots as the summer vegetables died down. I planted some very late (October) one year and didn't get any heads in the advertised 40 days (though I did get some very slow-growing leaves). However, the heads appeared in January during a bout of warm weather, and I was able to harvest a handful several times over the next few weeks. Tasty fried up with leftover boiled potatoes!

Sow direct, as with mustard greens, and harvest the heads as they appear. You can also eat the leaves.

Foraging and Wild Jellies

This time of year is great for foraging in parks and other green spaces. During the year I was writing this, we had a particularly good flowering season in the spring and thus a particularly good fruiting season in the autumn for plants like wild roses and hawthorn. Both rosehips and haws (hawthorn berries) make excellent jellies; you can also make rosehip syrup which is supposed to be good for sore throats. Rosehips are very high in Vitamin C, so if you have wild roses around, go gathering!

Rosehips should be picked once they're fully red, and ideally once they're slightly soft. You can make jam from hard rosehips picked in late September or early October, but if you want to make syrup, wait until November. (Having said that, some rosebushes ripen a little earlier, so adjust your picking time accordingly.) Haws are ready as soon as they're dark red. Both rosehips and haws can be eaten raw, but make sure not to eat the seeds of rosehips as they're an irritant (and bear in mind that the fruit is much tastier once it's soft).

When picking wild fruit or berries, make sure that you don't take all the berries; you should leave some for the birds and for the bush. Taking a third of what's there, if the bush is well-covered, is a good rule of thumb. Blackberries are also available wild at this time of year – check your local park, especially if you have a nearby river, as they do well near water. See p.183 for more on foraging and where you might be able to find free food plants in urban areas.

Make rosehip or hawthorn jelly as soons as possible after you've picked the fruit for maximum vitamin content. According to the recipes I read, rosehips should need added pectin to set properly. Mine set anyway after a fairly short boil, although it was a little runny (somewhere between honey and jelly). Haws contain plenty of their own pectin so there's no need to add any. You can also mix some haws with your hips to get a little pectin in there; or use a little apple (including the core and skin) or rhubarb, again for their pectin.

Hawthorn jelly is nice with cheese (or with cold meat if you eat meat), as a relish with lentil or nut roast, and on toast. It's a little bland all by itself; add apples to increase the interest. Rosehip jelly is lovely on toast.

You can also mix both hips and haws if you don't have enough of one for a decent quantity of jam. Be careful, when making either and especially when making small quantities, not to boil the juice and sugar for too long, or you'll get something more like toffee. Tasty, but hard to extract from a jar.

Rosehip or Hawthorn Jelly

1. Pick over the rosehips or hawthorns and wash them. You can if you wish cut off the brown tops of the hips, or if using haws, take the stalks off, but I don't bother since the juice will be strained anyway.

2. Boil the fruit in plenty of water for around an hour, mashing occasionally with a potato masher to break them up and help extract the juice. Don't let the pan boil dry!

3. Put the juice and pulp in a clean jelly bag, muslin, or pair of old tights, and let it strain into a bowl. I use the kitchen cupboard handles to suspend the jelly bag from. If you want a clear jelly, leave it to drip overnight and do not squeeze it. If, like me, you don't mind a slightly cloudy jelly, you can squeeze the pulp to extract the juice.

4. Optionally, boil up the pulp for another half an hour with some more water, and strain it again, to get the most out of the pulp. Put the pulp into the compost, and set the juice aside until you're ready to turn it into jelly (either immediately, or the next evening if you're pushed for time).

5. For each 500ml of juice, you normally need 450g of sugar. I found this a bit too sweet with the rosehip jelly, and made my second batch with 350g to a 500ml instead. Less sugar will affect how long it'll stay good for, however. Hawthorn was fine with just under 450g of sugar per 500ml of juice (although note that I don't have a very sweet tooth).

6. Bring the juice, sugar, and a good slosh of lemon juice to the boil, make sure the sugar has melted, and boil until it reaches setting point. To test for the setting point, put a plate in the fridge to get cold, then drop a little of the jelly mixture onto the plate and put it back into the fridge for two minutes. If it crinkles when you pull your finger across it, it's done.

7. Meanwhile, wash a few jars and put them (with their tops off) in a 100°C oven to sterilise them.

8. Fill the jars with the jelly, put a top on them (and ideally a waxed jam top paper under the lid), and label them. WARNING: glass jars just out of the oven stay hot for a long time. Be careful!

Yarrow

Yarrow is commonly seen growing wild, but it's a very pretty herb to grow in a garden or balcony as well. It's also known as millefoil and staunchweed, among other things. It's a perennial, so once established needs little looking after.

Growing

A month before sowing, wrap the seeds in a damp paper towel and place in the fridge in a sealed plastic bag. This helps to break the dormancy of the seeds and encourages them to grow. When sowing, place the seeds on the potting soil and lightly press them in, then put the pot somewhere brightly-lit (yarrow will not germinate in the dark). Seedlings take about 7 days to emerge, after which you should move the pot to a sunny windowsill. Keep the soil moist.

Transplant to a larger pot outside once the plants are 10-15cm tall. Keep the soil moist throughout spring, summer, and winter – although it's drought-tolerant, it does better in moist soil. There is no need to feed yarrow – as with the majority of wildflowers, it thrives on less-fertile soil, and can actually suffer from too much fertiliser being applied! Keep the pot in full sunshine.

Culinary uses

Yarrow isn't a particularly useful culinary herb – its uses are more medicinal (see below). However, the young leaves, which have a peppery and slightly bitter flavour, can be eaten in salad in the spring.

Medicinal uses

Traditionally, yarrow was used for wounds and minor bleeding (hence its names of staunchweed and bloodwort), to reduce digestive inflammation, and as a sedative. These days, it's used for menstrual pain and irregular menstruation, to reduce bleeding and heal wounds, to fight infection, and for indigestion.

The easiest way to take it is as a tea: steep 1-2 teaspoons of leaves or flowers in boiling water, and drink three times a day.

Yarrow growing wild in the grass.

You can also use extract or tincture from the flowers. Fill a jar with coarsely chopped flower tops, then fill the jar to the top with alcohol (vodka that is at least 50% alcohol by volume), and leave for six weeks. The tincture is useful to ward off colds (5-10 drops daily) or to treat them (a dropperful every 4 hours). You can also gargle with the tincture for a sore throat, or use it to wash a wound.

You can make yarrow oil from coarsely chopped leaves; again, fill a jar with dried leaves cut into 2.5cm long pieces, pour in olive oil to the top, and leave for six weeks before decanting the oil. A tissue damped with yarrow oil applied to the nose (be careful not to put it up too far!) can help with healing a nosebleed.

Yarrow contains essential oils including linalool and camphor. Test tube studies have found parts of yarrow oil to exhibit anti-inflammatory properties, and further animal studies have found that the alkoid 'achilletin' in yarrow stops bleeding, and that yarrow may also be liver protective. However, the scientific evidence is not currently conclusive, despite its long history of use in folk medicine.

Note that large doses taken regularly over a long time may make the skin sensitive to sunlight.

CHAPTER 12

OCTOBER

October is the time to tidy up your space after another successful season, leaving only your autumn and winter vegetables, and perennial herbs. Some herbs need to be moved into a cold frame around now, as well. And there's still scope for some more urban foraging.

· ·

My Balcony at the Start of October

Plants still alive and growing:

- **Tomatoes**, with a final few tomatoes still hanging on to ripen (as the weather was still good, I hadn't taken them off yet).
- **Herbs**: sage, mint, rosemary, bay, thyme, chives, oregano, basil, parsley, dill, papalo, coriander.
- **Rocket**, **mizuna**, and **bronze arrowhead lettuce** still cropping.
- Tiny fruit on the **pepper** plant at last!
- **Satsuma** tree – had to conclude that no crop was happening this year, sadly.

Seeds and cuttings:

- Self-seeded **basil** seedlings (just brought inside).
- Self-seeded **chive** seedlings.
- Self-seeded **bronze arrowhead lettuce** and **rocket** starting to appear. ⟶

Patience finally pays off: a pepper on the chilli pepper plant. It was very tasty; and the plant survived the following winter on the windowsill, too, so hopefully more will appear next year.

Things to Do in October

- Pull up and compost anything that's definitely dead.

- Pick the last few tomatoes (either leave them on a windowsill to ripen, or make green tomato chutney – see p.37).

- Get out the cold frame (p.178) if the weather deteriorates quickly.

- Bring in delicate herbs, if the weather deteriorates quickly.

- Harvest useful weeds (p.179).

The End of the Gardening Season
– nearly time for a rest!

In the northern hemisphere, autumn is traditionally the time to tidy up, protect any hardy plants that you may want to keep going through the winter, and put your feet up.

Tidying up isn't exactly the sexiest part of gardening, but it's nevertheless worth spending some time on it now. I find that in the spring I start off with good intentions; then before long the pace of events has overtaken me a little, and I'm shoving pots in anywhere they'll fit. The dog's intermittent 'help' doesn't improve this situation any, either.

Clearing up now means that when spring comes and you suddenly realise that it's time to start putting seeds into things, you're ready to go and don't have to waste sowing time in clearing up. It also gives you an opportunity to take stock of what's worked and what hasn't; what you'll definitely grown again, what isn't worth the hassle, and what you might have another go at and do slightly differently next year.

Stacking up your unused pots can also free you up to think again about how you use the space, if you've had them in a particular configuration for a while. One of the joys of gardening in containers is that you can easily move them around, but in my experience this is far less likely to happen when they're full of compost and dead plant roots. Take the opportunity to look at your emptier space, and make some decisions about how to plan it. There's more on planning in the Introduction.

As you're clearing out dead plants, collecting any remaining seeds, and even emptying the leftover compost in the pots back into a bag for revitalisation in the spring (see p.80), now is also a good chance to transfer any finished compost from your compost bin or wormery. It'll create space for the worms to process the dead material that you're throwing in there now. Be careful not to add too much woody material – see p.33 for more on compost balance and worm composting generally.

You can either mix the old and new compost up now (see p.22), or you can just leave the new compost in a bag in a spare corner. Make sure that the bag is sealed (with a small air hole or two) so that the compost doesn't dry out over the winter. Old shop-bought potting compost bags are good for this; or you can use a thick black plastic sack.

Tidying out your Seed Collection

Another job for this time of year is looking through any seeds you have left over. Most seeds (with the exception of carrots, which are definitely one season only) will keep for a second season, but after that the germination rate is likely to go down. To make sure that your seeds are still good, you can do a test germination. Take ten seeds and rinse them in clean water, then line them up on a damp paper towel and roll the towel around them. Put the whole lot in a zip-lock plastic bag, and leave them somewhere with suitable germination temperatures. Check daily to see whether any seeds have germinated. The test ends when either all seeds have germinated, or the maximum germination time (check the packet) has passed. If fewer than 60% of seeds germinate, this is probably the last season for that packet (and make a note on the packet to sow them thickly next spring!). Below 40% it's probably not worth keeping them.

However, if you do have some low-germination-rate seeds, it might be worth conducting some experiments with them before you throw them out. For some plants, it's just not feasible to get any growth out of them in the winter. (There's no real point in sowing sweet or chilli peppers, for example, which need high temperatures to germinate.) However, some seeds will do quite well over the winter, especially if your space is sheltered or south-facing. As on p.46, some plants are good for overwintering anyway; but if you have some spare seeds from other plants, why not try sowing them and see what happens? I have had good luck with autumn-sown broad beans (which will overwinter happily); and my bronze arrowhead lettuce self-seeded in September and October, with perfectly healthy seedlings appearing towards the end of October. You probably won't get the same yield that you would if sowing them in the 'proper' season, but you'll find out something interesting, and you may get an extra crop to cheer you up as the days draw in.

Succession Sowing through October

Rocket and bronze arrowhead lettuce will grow through October, as will some other greens such as mizuna. See p.84 for more on salad greens. If you let existing plants go to seed earlier in the season, they may well have self-seeded already. If you don't want the seedlings in the places where they've sown themselves, you can move them once they're established

Wine box and plank, to be used to create a cold frame.

Wine box with sloping plank upper section.

Cold frame with its plastic top on and plants inside.

(with at least two real leaves). Dig them up carefully, avoiding any disturbance in their roots, and move them elsewhere.

Chives and parsley are particularly good at self-seeding in my experience, but my basil, bronze arrowhead lettuce, and rocket all also regularly self-seed. I often leave them where they sowed themselves, if it's remotely convenient for me, on the grounds that clearly that space suits the seed or it wouldn't have germinated there!

Getting out the Cold Frame

Now is also a good time to either get out or construct a cold frame (see p.36). You'll also need to decide what must go in there to survive, what will produce better in the cold frame, and what can do without it.

Some varieties of lettuce are cold-hardy and will survive outside a cold frame, but they may crop slightly better with the shelter of the cold frame. I've found that bronze arrow head lettuce and rocket will both do well both inside and outside a cold frame, but you get slightly more tender leaves with a cold frame. Depending on the structure of the cold frame, however, the plants may also get a little less light and therefore get a bit more 'leggy'.

In terms of herbs, rosemary, sage, and thyme will all do fine out of a cold frame, but will stop growing until the spring. Oregano will die back if left outside unprotected (but will rejuvenate in the spring). Chives will die back whether or not they're in a cold frame (then, again, rejuvenate in the spring), so it's not really worth taking up the space. Basil and other very delicate plants need more warmth than that, so you'll need to take them inside or resign yourself to replanting in the spring.

It's also, as ever, worth experimenting. Wherever possible, sow one set of a type of plant outside and one inside the cold frame, and see what happens. The small, tougher leaves that rocket produces when left outside may be more to your taste than the larger, softer, less spicy ones that come out of the cold frame, for example. Or your space may have a warm enough corner that your rosemary will prefer being outside anyway. My rosemary this year was too big to fit in the cold frame. Despite the snow and long cold snap that we had in December in my area, I was able to (gently, and with restraint), crop from it throughout the winter. Rosemary and other Mediterranean plants can be surprisingly hardy; it can get very cold overnight and in the winter in places like Provence where they grow wild.

Useful Weeds

This is also the time of year for harvesting weeds such as chickweed (available throughout the winter; see p.47 for more) or dandelion. Dandelion leaves are tough and nasty at this time of year, but the roots are at their best, and can be dried and used to make dandelion tea.

You probably won't have any dandelions in your own patch if you're above ground level (although you might even in a paved space at ground level – dandelion seeds spread far and wide on the wind), but you can keep an eye out in local parks and on waste ground. Be careful that if a patch of land has been recently used for industrial purposes, eating roots from it may not be safe. Similarly, if picking low level weeds such as chickweed, be aware that inquisitive dogs, foxes, or cats may have been wandering around the area. (This is less of an issue for roots.) You should also avoid roadside areas which will be heavily polluted. Make sure you thoroughly wash anything you gather from public spaces.

When gathering wild plants, never take all the plants you see. It's important to leave enough there to sustain the population. It's reasonable to take up to around a third of what you see. Weeds in your own pots, of course, you can make your own decisions about (the likelihood of actually exterminating the lot is always pretty low, in my experience).

Dandelion root

Look for larger plants when digging, and dig carefully to get as much of the root as you can (dandelion roots can be huge).

Dandelion root decoction is supposed to have general tonic effects, and in particular to be good for the liver and kidneys. I have found it useful for perking one up if feeling slightly under the weather the morning after a couple of glasses of wine!

To dry dandelion root, chop the roots off the plants (throw the green leaves in the compost), wash them, and spread them out on a tea towel. Fold the tea towel over, and place them somewhere warm until entirely dried (this may take a few days). The airing cupboard is a good spot. Once dried, keep them in an airtight jar.

As dandelion roots are quite tough, you need to make a decoction rather than an infusion, which means that you simmer the roots on the stove in water for around 15 minutes. The decoction tastes pleasantly earthy, and (contrary to my expectations) not at all bitter. However, a spoonful of honey is a nice addition to it. Other herbal infusions or decoctions can be very nice as well – see the 'Herb of the Month' section at the end of each chapter for more on medicinal herbs.

Ginger

Strictly speaking, ginger is of course a spice rather than a herb, but it is too useful a winter root to leave out, and you may be surprised to know it can be grown in cool temperate climates. Growing your own ginger also makes it easy to experiment with green (young) ginger as well as the more common older root.

Growing

Ginger has to be an indoor plant in the UK or anywhere that has frosts, as it can't handle cold temperatures at all. It's a tropical plant, and likes shelter, warmth, humidity, and rich, moist soil. It gets on very badly with direct sun, strong wind, and waterlogged soil, and is not at all frost-hardy.

To grow it, look for fresh ginger in the shops in late winter or early spring, and choose a piece with a 'finger' which has a small pyramidal bud growing at its end. Soak it overnight, then cut off at least 5cm from this piece, and bury it bud-up in a 20cm pot of compost. Put the pot in a warm, sunny place. It must be kept warm and moist during the growing season, and the soil should be rich and free-draining (moist but not waterlogged is good!). As it starts to grow, feed every 2-3 weeks, and pot it on into larger pots as it grows.

You can start harvesting it from about four months' old, by digging at the side of a clump and breaking off the young, fresh rhizomes – these have a milder flavour than mature ginger (see below). In the autumn, once the leaves have died down, you can dig the whole thing up (easy if you're growing in a container!) and break up the rhizomes. Replant a few for next year (pick the ones with good growing buds), and use the rest for cooking.

Culinary uses

In cooking, it's the root of the plant that is used. The old root should be gathered when the stalk and leaves wither in autumn; the young roots can be harvested earlier, as above. Make sure not to harvest everything, or you won't have a plant next year!

Ginger shows up a lot in Asian and Chinese cooking. Spinach or other greens flash fried with garlic and ginger are lovely, and you can use ginger in a stir fry. Young roots (rhizomes) have a milder flavour than older roots, and, unlike older roots, can be used unpeeled. Young ginger is also what is used for candied ginger or stem ginger in syrup. The young roots will be pink-tipped, and are also known as green ginger or stem ginger.

Medicinal uses

Ginger is often used to counteract nausea in various situations (including motion sickness, pregnancy nausea, and some studies suggest it may help with chemotherapy-induced nausea). It's also used as an anti-inflammatory, and there's evidence that it can help with arthritis. You can simply use it in cooking, or try chopping or grating it finely then steeping or boiling it in water to make a tea.

CHAPTER 13

ZONES 4 AND 5 THE WIDER URBAN ENVIRONMENT

In permaculture terminology, zone 4 refers to rough grazing and woodland, and zone 5 to wilderness; they're the zones furthest from the central point (usually your home). In an urban environment, we don't really have either of those things (indeed, in a country like Britain, there's hardly any real 'wilderness' at all). You can think of your own zone five provision as being things like bug boxes (see p.132), or plants which are there primarily to attract insects (see p.116). They do have benefits for you, but those are really a positive side effect of the advantage that they give to the wild insects. Of course, plants with multiple benefits are a very permaculture thing anyway!

Another way of thinking about zones four and five in the urban environment, though, is to look at all the areas outside your direct sphere of influence; the urban jungle. What is there out there for the balcony permaculturist?

Urban Wild Food Foraging

Even in urban areas, there is a surprising amount of free wild food available in parks and other green spaces (such as a shared garden square on an estate, for example, or public municipal flower beds that have been taken over by the odd weed; or disued lots if you can get into them), if you know what to look for.

There are two classes of land where you might find food: public (usually council owned) and private. The legality of harvesting wild food on public land is a little unclear. On the one hand, arguably if the land is publicly funded, it belongs to the public; on the other hand, technically it probably belongs to the landowner (usually the local council) rather than to whoever pays for the council (everyone). In practice, you're unlikely to get into trouble on public land if you act sensibly and politely.

It's more clearly illegal to harvest wild food on private land that isn't yours. Even if all you're after is the weeds, private landowners may take a dim view of people trespassing on their property. If the possible bounty is worth it, make sure you keep an eye out for security firms who may be sceptical about your motives, and/or get the permission of the landowner first. As with guerrilla gardening. With weeds in particular, you're really not taking anything of any value, so you may get away with it anyway. If you see a fruit tree in a private garden with no sign that anyone's harvesting the crop, you could try knocking on the door and offering a deal whereby you'll pick the fruit in exchange for a share of it. (Or a jar or two of quince jam from the quince tree you spot in someone's hedge, or...). It may even be the start of a beautiful friendship. If, on the other hand, all you want is a few leaves from the lime tree, or flowers from the elderflower, that's hanging over the fence onto the pavement, you may as well just help yourself.

It's important to be aware that any land you don't have control over, including parks or other public spaces, may have chemical fertilisers or pesticides that you don't know about used on the plants. The more heavily manicured and managed the land looks, the more likely this is, so use your judgement. Also, low hanging fruit (or anything on the ground) may have been christened by passing dogs/foxes/humans. Again, use your judgement, and always wash anything you've foraged before eating it. Plants growing near to roads (especially busy roads) may gather a patina of exhaust fumes. Again, wash before eating, and you may want to avoid foraging around obviously very polluted areas (e.g. roundabouts, which sometimes have little wild or cultivated patches on them, are almost certainly not worth it as they will be heavily polluted).

Fruit

Probably the best known and most often foraged wild fruit in the UK are blackberries, which run rampant wherever they're given the opportunity. In fact, blackberries are grown all over the world in pretty much every suitable temperate climate.

Brambles are often found near rivers, and rare is the park or green space that hasn't acquired a blackberry patch somewhere (partly because they're damn hard to get rid of). Wild blackberries tend to taste better than domesticated ones, so even if you have a garden chances are you'll be better off going out looking for blackberries elsewhere rather than planting your own. (Also, blackberries can be a bit of a menace to manage in a small garden as they are highly dedicated to spreading themselves everywhere.) I remember blackberrying in our local park as a child growing up in suburban London, and taking ice cream tubs full of fruit home to put in the freezer and turn into blackberry and apple crumble. Blackberrying is pretty much a UK institution – go forth and seek your own! As well as the summer/autumn fruit, you can also eat the young leaves of brambles in the spring, either as a salad, or cooked.

Other fruits are also available if you keep your eyes open. Apple trees aren't as common in the UK as they are in other European countries (in Prague in September everyone is after the apples from the trees in the park), but they do exist, especially in neglected private gardens (ask rather than scrumping!). In southern England you'll see huge numbers of cherry trees everywhere, which are grown for their blossom. Many of these are flowering cherries which don't really produce fruit, but not all of them are limited to looking pretty. There's a cherry tree on my estate which produces tiny sweet cherries, well worth picking even to nibble on despite the fact that there's more stone than flesh. Some parks have plum or damson trees in, too.

Sweet chestnuts are common in parks (Hyde Park has a large number along the bike path south of the Serpentine), and you can harvest these at the right time of the year, deshell them (a spiky business, so watch your fingers!) and roast them.

Another fruit tree worth looking out for is the fig. Fig trees grow well in the southern UK and in most reasonably temperate climates. They prefer warm and dry, but they're also cold-hardy, and they're sometimes grown decoratively. There's a fig tree in the grounds of the Palace of Westminster in London which grows over the fence and into the street – so if you've ever fancied eating Parliamentary fruit, head down there at the right time of year!

Less well known, but perhaps more readily available, wild fruits are rosehips and hawthorns, both of which make very nice jelly (see p.171). Both can also be eaten raw, although be careful not to swallow the seeds of the rosehips, as they're an irritant and can make you quite unwell. Hawthorn is grown everywhere (often as a hedge) and you are unlikely to have any problems finding some, nor is anyone likely to care if you pick a few berries. Young (spring) hawthorn leaves are also edible raw.

Picking fruit in public spaces does require a certain willingness to perhaps look a bit peculiar, but the results are well worth any momentary embarrassment.

Fungi

There are many mushrooms and other fungi growing wild in all sorts of places in the UK and elsewhere. Some of them are not only edible, but delicious.

If you're interested in mushroom gathering, your best bet is to find someone who already knows their stuff, and go along on a few expeditions with them. You should also invest in a good reference book with plenty of pictures, but there's no substitute for experience. **None** of the old folk wisdom about mushrooms are true: being able to peel them doesn't guarantee edibility, nor does colour (poisonous mushrooms and edible toadstools both exist!), nor does the smell. The **only** way to confirm that a particular fungus is edible is to make a definite identification of its species.

WARNING Some mushrooms and fungi are poisonous, in some cases fatally so. Don't take risks – make sure you are certain of your identification and, if in doubt, don't eat.

If in doubt, don't eat. Even very competent mushroom hunters have been known to make a mistake and fetch up in hospital (or worse). But there are very tasty fungi out there, so don't be put off altogether – just do your homework.

Greenery

As well as the more obvious fruit and fungi, there are also many edible 'weeds'. Chickweed (see p.47), dandelions (for either spring leaves or autumn roots, see p.180), rocket (not as common as the others, but I've seen it growing as a weed in pavement cracks), nettle (wash and cook like spinach), fat hen (eat whole plant as salad or cook like spinach), and yarrow (eat raw, or cook like spinach, but remove the stems first as they're stringy) are all edible.

As already discussed, the main thing to be careful of is to think about what animals or pollution might have affected the plants; and also to consider whether the ground itself might be industrially polluted. My local park has been there for over 150 years, so I'm happy that the ground there is clear enough, but some abandoned areas may have had pollutants spilled or even buried there.

Other Urban Foraging

Foraging isn't just limited to food. There's a wide and exciting array of things that you can find around you for free or close to free.

Skips can be a great source of timber (especially pallets), empty plastic tubs (check what they used to contain and wash thoroughly before using to grow anything in), and other interesting bits and pieces. Technically in the UK the contents of a skip still legally belong to whoever owns or hired it, but in practice, again, you're unlikely to get into trouble. If the skip is in someone's front garden, or you see the builders or whoever around, it's best to check with them that they don't mind (but they're unlikely to – you're doing them a favour by saving them having to pay for dumping it somewhere!). Skips at the back of supermarkets may contain nearly out of date or out of date but still edible produce, as well, but that's slightly outside the scope of this book. Google for 'freeganism' to find out more.

Freecycle or **Freegle** are online ventures (usually run via email list, sometimes via a website or forum) where you can give stuff you don't want to nearby people who need it, and get hold of stuff other people don't want, all for free. You'll usually have to collect things yourself, although the offerer may be prepared to post lighter things. Be warned that desirable stuff goes very fast, so if you're after anything specific, you'll have to keep a close eye on the list. As well as watching for people getting rid of useful stuff, you can ask for specific things. This will go better if you've contributed yourself before (clear out all those belongings that are still good but you don't want or use any more), and if you don't take the piss. "Anyone got any spare plant pots?" and "Anyone got a games console they're not using?" are two very different queries.

Charity shops are another good way of getting rid of things (better than Freecycle because you can often get rid of the lot all at once; worse because you have to carry it down there) and picking up bargains.

Look out for cheap saucers to go under your plant pots! Note that some charity shops won't take second-hand electrical goods, call first to find out.

Free shops are a bit like a cross between Freecycle and a charity shop. People take their unwanted stuff along, and other people who want it take it away (for free). They usually operate out of social centres (often squatted spaces), and may not last very long. At the time of writing I knew of one in Camberwell and one in Hackney but by the time this is in print they'll be operating elsewhere if at all. Check out websites like www.indymedia.co.uk to find this sort of thing.

Other People and Other Spaces

You can do a lot for yourself by yourself, but the impact you can have on your local food web is likely to be fairly limited. If you're interested in making wider changes, you can reach out to bigger spaces and to your neighbours.

Guerrilla gardening

Guerrilla gardening is about challenging the idea that a 'garden' has to be something owned by a particular person or organisation. Richard Reynolds, author of *On Guerrilla Gardening*, who lives and gardens in Elephant and Castle, London (a few minutes' bike ride from me), defines it as "the illicit cultivation of someone else's land". Guerrilla gardeners don't wait for permission to plant; they go ahead and garden in any place where it looks like there's a neglected space which could benefit from someone tending it. It's about creating gardens – whether those are tiny patches of flowers, or huge multi-person endeavours on large areas – where there was previously just neglect. The first self-defined guerrilla gardeners were New Yorkers on the Lower East Side in the 1970s, creating community gardens on abandoned lots. These have in a lot of cases since been legitimised, and are now beautiful well-established oases of green in a very urban area.

If the idea of guerrilla gardening inspires you to spread a little horticultural joy in your own area, you can start small: perhaps at the foot of a tree, or in a neglected-looking public flowerbed. If you already have seeds for your own space, you can undoubtedly spare a few to throw in elsewhere; or you can pick up a tiny packet of wildflower seeds or a handful of bulbs. (Wildflowers are particularly good for guerrilla gardening as they tend to thrive on poor soil.) Flowers that self-seed are good for minimal maintenance, but make sure you don't plant anything too invasive (mint, for example) if it might spread elsewhere or further than you want. Be especially careful with anything non-native. Bulbs are another good low maintenance choice, and will keep coming back year on year.

One neat trick for poor soil, or if you want to be able to just drop the seeds and go, is to create 'seed bombs'. These are little balls of seeds and earth/compost, which you can drop or even throw onto the area you're aiming for. The earth will give the seeds a start, after which they can dig themselves into wherever they land.

If you want to take things further – maybe there's a long-term derelict lot round the corner from you that you would love to see become a community resource rather than an eyesore – you'll probably need to get other people involved at some point. Check out Richard Reynolds' book for more suggestions and inspiration.

You could also consider doing a little guerrilla land regeneration and detoxification, if you have some spare compost tea (see p.123). Most urban soil is heavily polluted by years of traffic fumes if nothing else. The single best way to detoxify soil is long-term organic gardening, adding plenty of organic matter over time and allowing that to clean the land, but a short-term way to help this out is to apply compost tea. Especially if you want to grow food plants in your reclaimed/guerrilla gardened area, this is probably worth doing to improve the soil quality quickly.

Community gardens and orchards

Community gardens are one way of reclaiming unused space. If there's a green area near your block of flats or estate, see if the council are up for a group of you taking it over and making it more beautiful and/or more productive. If you're setting up a group to do this, or trying to get other residents involved, look for some quick wins early on to encourage everyone. Anything that grows fast and is tasty is good! Lettuce, peas, and tomatoes may all be a good choice, depending on the time of year. Over time you can observe the space and plan it better (and, hopefully, with guidance from permaculture principles). You may even be able to get some form of council funding.

Look out for other sorts of open private space, too. The Castle indoor climbing centre in north London has started a food garden a couple of years ago which, at the time of writing, is doing very well.

Community orchards work on the same principle but with fruit trees. As a rule, their main purpose is not the production of fruit (although that is a major benefit!), but the provision of a space for the community to enjoy. This means that they can be managed with an eye to *all* the benefits of an orchard (including education, beauty, and a place for local people to spend time) rather than focussing solely on how much fruit is generated. Tasty fruit for local people to harvest is a great bonus to having an orchard rather than just a park, though! Have a look online to see if there's an orchard in your area.

If you can't set up a garden or orchard with the landowner's permission, the other alternatives include guerrilla gardening (as discussed above) or squatting a space (as the Transition Towns Heathrow group did in Sipton in 2010). The downside to squatting is of course the risk of getting kicked off the land just when you're getting things going, but if you put the energy into getting local residents involved, you may be able to keep it. The Grow Heathrow project was able to stay much longer than they expected, with a strong and supportive local campaign. The longer the landowner has left the land derelict, the more organised you are, and the more local support you have, the better your chances.

Nature Reserves

Nature reserves both large and small exist in many cities, and are another possible outreach option. If you have a nature reserve nearby, you could get involved with the group maintaining it, and see if there's interest in integrating a permaculture/wild food section into it. Permaculture is all about promoting beneficial webs and local wildlife, so this is definitely possible (although not everyone may go for it). I'm currently involved with doing this at my local nature reserve in Bermondsey. Be aware that nature reserves are wildlife habitats **not** allotments, and should not be seen as primarily a food source.

City Farms

City farms are another project you can get involved with, and which may be interested in having either a permaculture corner, or adopting a more traditional allotmenting approach, or a mix of the two. Again, go along, talk to people, and find out what's going on and what you can get involved in.

Other Options

Transition Towns and other similar local movements are a possibility for getting in touch with other people with similar interests, and seeing what you might be able to start up together. You could also consider working with schools, old people's homes, hospitals... anywhere that has open space and might be interested in doing something different with even a small corner of it. Does your workplace have a balcony or a roof? You could ask permission to stick a few pots up there and start a tomato plantation.

On a more local level, your **neighbours** may have a garden and not have the time to look after it or know where to start. You could offer to look after their garden in return for planting up a section of it; or help them to get started themselves.

Finally, if you really want more space all of your own, put yourself down for an **allotment**. Inner city allotments often have long waiting lists; a bit further out of town you may be a bit luckier. Occupy yourself during the wait by planning what you'll do with it once you get it...

RESOURCES

Seed Providers

The following providers do organic seeds by mail order in the UK:

The Real Seed Catalogue
All their seeds are organic, non-GM, non-hybrid and breed true.
www.realseeds.co.uk
Real Seeds, PO Box 18, Newport near Fishguard,
Pembrokeshire SA65 0AA .
Tel: 01239 821 107.

Organic Gardening Catalogue
All organic, some hybrid.
www.organiccatalog.com / catalog
The Organic Gardening Catalogue, Riverdene Business Park,
Molesey Road, Hersham, Surrey KT12 4RG.
Tel: 01932 253 666.

Tamar Organics
All organic.
www.tamarorganics.co.uk
Cartha Martha Farm, Rezare, Launceston, Cornwall PL15 9NX.
Tel: 01579 371 182.

PICTURE ACKNOWLEDGEMENTS

Cover, Maddy Harland; worms, pp.31, 126, Zbyszek Nowak/Fotolia; mug rings, pp.32, 81, 197, Axel Bückert/Fotolia; shredded paper, pp.33, 100, Jakub Krechowicz/ Fotolia; soil, pp.34, 80, 119, Sergey Galushko/Fotolia; wirebound pad, pp.37, 159, 171, patpitchaya/Fotolia; herb collection, pp.41, 42, 52, 53, 67, 68, 77, 103, 125, 136, 145, 153, 163, 173, 182, robynmac/Fotolia; individual herbs, pp.41, 52, 76, 102, 144, Barbara Pheby, Fotolia; notepaper, pp.49, 122, 132, picsfive/Fotolia; seed packets, p.55, triffitt,/iStockphoto; seeds, pp.57, 96, 130, 135, 158, 177, BamBamImages/ iStockphoto; individual herbs, pp. 67, 152, Elena Schweitzer/Fotolia; watering can, pp.73, 114, 140, Elenathewise/Fotolia; pp.91, 116, 172, ksena32/Fotolia; 92, JF Gicquel/Fotolia; p.95, pixelunikat/Fotolia; minted potatoes, p.101, Colinda McKie/ Fotolia; p.117, ella/Fotolia; p.118, unpict/Fotolia; p.120, reflux/Fotolia; p.121, Ruud Morijn/Fotolia; p.137, scis65/Fotolia; p.154, Jopelka/Shutterstock; p.155, Skowron/ Shutterstock; p.166, Picture Partners/Fotolia; p.168, Maksim Shebeko/Fotolia; p.170, ppfoto13/Fotolia; p.181, myfotolia88/Fotolia. All other images are the author's copyright.

Inspiration for
Designing a Better World

Permaculture magazine helps you live a more natural, healthy and environmentally friendly life.

Permaculture magazine offers tried and tested ways of creating flexible, low cost approaches to sustainable living, helping you to:

- Make informed ethical choices
- Grow and source organic food
- Put more into your local community
- Build energy efficiency into your home
- Find courses, contacts and opportunities
- Live in harmony with people and the planet

Permaculture magazine is published quarterly for enquiring minds and original thinkers everywhere. Each issue gives you practical, thought provoking articles written by leading experts as well as fantastic ecofriendly tips from readers!

permaculture, ecovillages, ecobuilding, organic gardening, agroforestry, sustainable agriculture, appropriate technology, downshifting, community development, human-scale economy ... and much more!

Permaculture magazine gives you access to a unique network of people and introduces you to pioneering projects in Britain and around the world. Subscribe today and start enriching your life without overburdening the planet!

PERMANENT PUBLICATIONS
The Sustainability Centre, East Meon, Hampshire GU32 1HR, UK
Tel: 01730 823 311 Fax: 01730 823 322   (Overseas: int code +44-1730)
Email: info@permaculture.co.uk

To subscribe and for daily updates, vist our exciting and dynamic website:
www.permaculture.co.uk

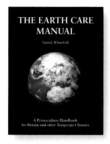